Television:
The Director's Viewpoint

Also in This Series

Big Story: How the American Press and Television Reported and Interpreted the Crisis of Tet 1968 in Vietnam and Washington, Peter Braestrup

Westview Special Studies in Communications

Television: The Director's Viewpoint
John W. Ravage

Television directors remain an enigma to most students of the mass media; traditionally, their function has been little understood by scholars and the viewing public. In this book, John Ravage studies the role of the director in the producer-dominated medium of commercial television. Built around lengthy interviews with twelve of the leading directors of commercial programs—representing all the genres of "prime time"—the book analyzes the major issues facing television, its past, present, and portents for the future, and the audience that watches it.

John W. Ravage is assistant professor of broadcasting at the University of Wyoming. He has worked in commercial radio and television, written for television, and recently worked at Universal Studios in California.

Television:
The Director's Viewpoint

John W. Ravage

Westview Press / Boulder, Colorado

Westview Special Studies in Communications

Copyright © 1978 by Westview Press

Published in 1978 in the United States of America by
  Westview Press, Inc.
  5500 Central Avenue
  Boulder, Colorado 80301
  Frederick A. Praeger, Publisher

Library of Congress Cataloging in Publication Data
Ravage, John W.
  The television director.
  (Westview special studies in communications)
  Includes index.
  1. Television—Production and direction. 2. Television broadcasting—United States.
I. Title.
PN1992.75.R34   791.45'0233   78-3789
ISBN 0-89158-337-8

Printed and bound in the United States of America

To Linda—my best friend

Contents

Preface

This work required nearly eighteen months to complete. Over that period, many came to my aid with suggestions and insights. I am especially grateful to Dr. Gage Chapel for his help, advice, and conversation.

In addition, special attention should be drawn to the aid which the University of Wyoming gave me through the Arts and Sciences Basic Research Program.

In writing this book, I talked with a large number of professionals in addition to those whose interviews are included in the text. Whatever insights exist in this work are largely a distillation of the observations of these film and video professionals. They include: Danny Arnold, producer and director; Nicholas Baehr, writer; Billy Barty, actor; Ron Carey, actor; John Chulay, director; Fielder Cook, director; Ivan Dixon, actor and director; Jaime Farr, actor; Ron Glass, actor; Dwight Hemion, director; Ted Knight, actor; Bob Lally, director; Richard Levinson, producer and writer; Bill Link, producer and writer; Jerry Markus, director; Jeff Melman, assistant director; Harry Morgan, actor; Jay Sandrich, director; Isabel Sanford, actress; Pat Shields, director; Loretta Swit, actress; and George Thompson, director.

Whatever shortcomings are apparent in this book are my responsibility. The insights derive from the evaluations and observations of the above-listed people.

Introduction

Commercial television compels the largest mass audience of any dramatic format in history. Ordinarily, 10 to 20 million viewers will watch one program; in 1978, 86 million watched the Super Bowl in January. Not surprisingly, groups appraise the content of programming with evaluations ranging from "excellent" to "terrible," the negative terms being predominant. Philosophers, politicians, social historians, and ordinary viewers protest programs. Few come to the defense of television.

The purpose of this book is neither to defend nor to attack contemporary television; the medium is far too diverse to be approached in such a facile manner. Instead, this text searches for an insight into television production derived from an insider's perspective—that of the television director.

The television director is generally unrecognized by audiences, even though they may be familiar with the major directors of motion pictures. This fact alone says much about the transitory nature of most television, a dramatic form which stresses quantity and popularity above all other concerns.

Directors, however, control the form and emphases of programs to an extent approached by few other members of a production. For that reason it seems valid to seek the views of these professionals to help illuminate various pressing issues in television today.

This is a study of commercial television, rather than of public broadcasting, cable communications, or educational/instructional programming. Commercial, network television is the primary entertainment form of our time. As yet, the audience for public and special-interest broadcasting does not approach that of the commercial networks. The directors, actors, writers, and producers interviewed for this book represent the main dramatic formats of network television—situation comedy and melodrama. News, public affairs, and children's and daytime programs are not represented. The directors on which this work focuses vary widely in age, training, temperament, and sensitivity. There is no single approach to either direction or production, and these people's works and perspectives are varied.

To all those who wish to understand more about the content of today's television, and the motivations of networks, advertisers, producers, writers, and actors, the views of these directors should be important; they contain unique perceptions of this, the most popular entertainment device of our times.

1
The Milieu of American Television

The center of American television lies at the southern extreme of the San Andreas fault, in the Los Angeles area. Ninety percent of what the American television networks produce is created at this point.

The impact of televised material upon the nation is enormous —greater than that of any other mass medium in our society. Children grow up imitating the heroes and heroines of television. Housewives trace out the days of their lives on the soap operas. Colleges and universities assemble programs of study for careers in television, for which their students have a ridiculously low chance of employment. In short, we are mesmerized by those images on the flickering cathode-ray tube, hypnotized to a degree that has changed our politics, our entertainment, and our self concepts.

Before any study of television may begin, it seems imperative that the organizational structures and patterns of commercial television should be understood, since few people except those who work in or study "the business" are conversant with the managerial and production elements of the medium.

The Production Company

Almost all commercial television programming comes from a "production organization" like Twentieth Century Fox, Universal City Studios, or Mary Tyler Moore Productions. These organizations produce programs funded either by the television networks or independently. First, a producer (working alone or as an employee of a production company) must convince a network or independent company to fund the production of a program or series. This may be a "television movie" (a one-and-a-half-hour or longer, non-series program), a "special" (a long-form movie-like production), or a "series pilot" (an open-ended dramatic structure which can form the basis for a regular, usually weekly, series). The network or production company allots a sum of money—typically, a million dollars or more for a series pilot—for the production. If the program is popular, they will assign whatever sum of money the producer is able to convince them to spend for a complete series. In most cases, a one-hour series segment will cost approximately $500,000.

Whether a production company or network is financing the pilot, movie, or special, it is the producer who has had to drum up financial support. His position is tenuous, based as it is upon his record in prognosticating public interest in his programs.

Because the entire industry is suspicious of change and familiar with the workings of production companies, only on very rare occasions are independent producers successful in securing contracts for television programs. (An independent is anyone not contractually allied with a formal production company.) Ironically, if independent producers do secure such a commitment from the networks, they invariably form their own production companies, which then often become as difficult to break into as the organizations which excluded their founders.

Once a production is financed, the producer—now called the "executive producer"—selects an immediate subordinate, the "producer." This line officer becomes the chief day-to-day controller of the project. He or she hires directors, casts the lead actors (in conjunction with the executive producer), supervises writing and rewriting, oversees the budget, and assures a continuing level of quality in the series.

The executive producer usually busies himself at this point with procuring new ideas for other series. Only occasionally does he visit the producer's office. In many cases, the executive producer reserves his final judgment on the release of a film or tape to the network until the conclusion of shooting.

The Director

In the mid-1800s the term "director" was unknown, at least in the sense that it is used in theater. Stage actors—a scorned and piteous lot—were like their productions: poorly organized and transient. Historically the company's lead actor was the "giver of parts, lines, and stage places." In the late 1800s a new occupation was created by the Austrian duke of Saxe-Meiningen—that of one who oversees the art and craft of a production. He was not merely a peer; he became manager of the various parts of a production.

Today, the term "director" is well known to high school thespians and the most casual moviegoers. In fact, since François Truffaut and Andrew Sarris drew the public's attention to the concept of *auteur,* we have been a nation (and world) fascinated by directors like Alfred Hitchcock, John Ford, and Francis Coppola. We have become *aficionados* of directing in film.

Unfortunately, the term "director" is weak in English. As a result, theorists and audiences alike strive to differentiate between "directors" of costuming, music, makeup, scene design, cinematography, editing, and all the crafts of film and videotape making. As an occupation, however, directing is clear cut. Once the $4,000 initiation fee is paid to the Directors' Guild of America and a contract to direct is signed, one is, per se, a director.

The Television Director—The Beginnings

"Most people don't know what a television director is *or* what he does," says director Buzz Kulik. Born in the early days of network broadcasting, television directing was a child of necessity. In the late 1940s the need for directors in this new medium was phenomenal. In New York City—then the center of all network production—most theatrical directors spurned the electronic medium as an upstart, a prostitution of good theater and talent for commercial ends. Therefore, stations looked wherever they could for their talent. Directors were found in the crafts of broadcasting: acting, editing, writing.

Today, television directors still come from a variety of backgrounds. Some, like Jack Shea and Noam Pitlik, were originally actors; others, like Pat Shields, were film editors; Walter Doniger began as a writer; Dan Petrie taught and acted.

The techniques of directing were as much created as learned by the earliest network directors like Paul Bogart, Fielder Cook, and

Boris Sagal. There was no time or place to study "technique."

As television grew in economic strength and pervasiveness, a second generation of directors was produced. The typical second generation director began as a college actor and then worked in off-Broadway (or off-Hollywood) productions. He (they were nearly all men) then gravitated to writing, editing, or acting in television or motion pictures. When he became convinced that there was little chance for him to become the *enfant terrible* of Hollywood, he looked to other employment opportunities. Often, television was the answer.

Other directors of this era were the sons and daughters of union members in southern California. They found it relatively easy to follow their parents' footsteps into film work. Some of the best-known contemporary directors emulate their parents: Jay Sandrich and Alan Alda, for example.

Regardless of their backgrounds, most directors were first attracted by motion pictures rather than television. As Paul Bogart tells it, they were children of the films—hoping upon hope that they would someday make it to the top. Some did; most didn't. They were drawn by that primal delight in performance that motivates all actors and most playwrights.

The realities of employment settled quickly upon those nascent talents. There are, after all, only about 25,000 persons employed in all the aspects of filmmaking (motion picture and television) in the United States. Most of these people were born in and around Los Angeles. The lack of opportunity in filmmaking was, and is, apparent to all who try to gain employment in the field. Therefore, many aspirants either abandoned their quest or lowered their sights and took jobs in allied professions, if they could find them.

The more successful (or luckier) aspiring directors found work in television series, all the while hoping for a chance to work in films. If they were fortunate enough to convince producers to hire them more than once or twice, they became permanent adjuncts to the television production teams. Later, if they continued to please their employers, they might work in long-forms like pilots or movies for television. Ultimately, they might still be hoping that a motion picture contract would result. For most it never did, and still doesn't.

Many of the television directors interviewed for this book work in both television and theatrical-release films: Lamont Johnson and John Badham, for example. All the rest expressed the desire to direct films.

Since it is obvious that not all television directors can work in motion pictures, one is tempted to ask why they persevere. At least, what are the differences that draw them to film? It is in the answer to this last question that the core of the art or craft of television direction can be found.

Television is, to these craftsmen, a "service" medium, one which functions to support the commercial interests of networks and advertisers. In Ivan Dixon's words, "My job is to put on film what the producer has realized." And the producer has realized a plan to stay employed by pleasing his employers, the networks.

Commercial television is simply a means to sell merchandise, a device to catch the audience's attention. It was not constituted on any lofty plane. Creativity, in John Badham's view, is "given up in order to keep employed." It was not always so. "Sixteen years ago the director was an important part of the creative process; it's no longer so," says Fielder Cook. The creative component is now the prerogative of the producer. The director is a temporary employee, a permanent itinerant.

The Director's Job

A director is hired by either the executive producer or the producer of a program, depending upon its format. In long-form production, the director is often part of the executive producer's original plan for the program, and is picked specially for the premiere episode. In series television, the director is often merely one of a changing parade of men and women who work on only one or two episodes per year.

Once the director is chosen, he has to perform three distinct operations: pre-production, shooting, and post-production. Each has its separate demands.

In pre-production (six days for a typical one-hour program and three to four days for a half-hour episode), the director meets with the executive producer and the producer for their views on the series and the segment at hand. Together, they determine the casting of supporting characters. (The lead actors are permanent.) In these sessions, the director—in consultation with the producer—chooses the appropriate set designs, costumes, make-up, and other theatrical elements necessary to the program. The shooting schedule is planned to take advantage of minimum costs for actors and rental of stages and equipment.

The actual shooting or videotaping of a program will consume from a half-hour, for a situation comedy taped in front of an audience, to six days, for a one-hour, filmed program. The filming or taping of the program comes after a rehearsal period of one day (for filmed programs) or two to four days (for situation comedy). Since the "live/taped" programs consume fewer shooting days, more time is added to rehearsing.

Post-production involves the director, producer, and executive producer in the cutting of the program to fit the actual running time for that segment. "One-hour" programs contain approximately forty-one to forty-three minutes of dramatic content. Half-hour episodes contain twenty to twenty-three minutes of material. Besides merely lengthening (by adding deleted bits of film or tape) or shortening the running time, the director may have to delete stray noises, add "off-camera" dialogue, "sweeten" the laugh track on comedies, or cover mistakes in camera angles, exposures, or dialogue.

The director who can master the exigencies of this production cycle—one who can bring it in on time and under the cost estimate—is deemed effective by producers and networks alike. One who consistently runs over budget or time (in search of quality) does not work long in commercial television.

With the rise of commercial content and the decline of creative programming, the television director lost what little chance he had to instill his artistic persona into his product, as stage and film directors do. Instead, he became a pragmatist, one who must, in Ivan Dixon's words, "be able to deal with the realities of television or get out. You do what you have to."

Doing what one "has to" means different things to different directors. To some it means realizing the limitations implicit in creating a product whose ultimate purpose is to generate an effective sales climate. In addition, as Joan Darling states, "in casting, hiring, and firing—the producer is your superior." The director is limited in his or her sense of theater by the producer's and the network's dictates. Neither can he reject many assignments and expect to stay in the business.

To the series director, compromise is constant. He demands less of actors and writers in order not to spend too much time or money—which are the same thing in this context—on completing a program. The director finds that less than perfectly cast actors must be cajoled and flattered into learning their lines or blocking. "It's part of the director's job," says Dan Petrie. The director may find that he must spend inordinate amounts of energy in the creation of a relaxed environment for wounded egos.

Not all directors see their job as that of an unappreciated artist in a field of tasteless barbarians—be they producers or actors. Instead, directors can view their work as "interpretive . . . sensitive to what the writer wants," in Gene Reynolds' words. Still others, such as Jack Shea, see the director as one who "instills confidence in a cast." "A television director's job is to help others see the material in the best possible way," says Paul Bogart.

There is little doubt that any director, in television, film, or the theater, is a collaborative worker. In the production of most television fare there is a constant interchange among actors, writers, crew, and producers—all intent upon making a program which will not run over its budget. All wish to remain employed.

In order to achieve that end, a program must join the actors and the script in such a way as to please audiences, producers, and the network. Since the creative control of content is the prerogative of others, the director searches for fulfillment where he can find it.

He often makes a game of his job, delighting in the mastery of technical skills and creative short cuts that will not consume too much time. "The fun is in solving problems," says Pat Shields. He masters the fine points of lighting, camera work, lenses, makeup and costuming. He may see his main interests as helping his actors find the strongest character identifications possible or as making a "happy family" out of his cast. It is in this way that he can sublimate his drive to do work of any depth—an outlet denied him by the production cycle.

Since technology is an integral part of television directing, the skills necessary to master the electronic marvels are compelling to many directors. They enjoy the chance to enhance performances and scripts by the manipulation of gadgetry—"to make performances look better than they are," as Fielder Cook relates. This seems not to be a perversion of the directorial process, but a legitimate goal of any artist practicing in any medium.

Both those who find fulfillment in television and those who do not seem to agree on its limitations. There is little room for the *auteur* style of direction. There are few visual or syntactical trademarks setting one television director off from another. A good show becomes its own reward, and the wise director lets it go at that. When a script and its production are truly superior, the director rejoices, but he must realize the transitory nature of his product. Then he can say, with Jay Sandrich, "I have been satisfied emotionally and intellectually by my work."

Television versus Film Directing

The press of the production cycle is apparent to all who work in television. Therefore, directors search for ways to use their time to maximum benefit. As Walter Doniger says, they must concentrate on "self-discipline and speed of decisions." They work long hours—often from 8 A.M. to near midnight—in order to extract the best performances possible. In motion pictures, time (and its associated costs) is certainly important, but schedules are more flexible. A feature may have to be completed in "approximate" time (allowing for such variables as weather, illness, script changes); a television program is allotted six days or less. There are few exceptions. Time is, then, the major physical and psychological restriction upon television productions. Time means one thing—money: money for crews who might have to work overtime, for extra stage rentals, for extra equipment.

Directors find that much of their energy is expended in trying to compensate for the time and money differences between films and television. Lamont Johnson remarks that he must organize far more tightly for television than for films. In addition, he finds that he must work with a sense of the wholeness of a production that is not always necessary in film: he must know *all* the ramifications of script and character so that time will not be lost in on-the-set character analysis and searching for motivations.

Hal Cooper, like Lamont Johnson, stresses preparation, the careful planning of all dramatic elements to take advantage of the time available. John Badham has found himself shooting shorter masters to avoid the languorous camera-movements that consume film—and actual—time.

In this search for efficiency, much is sacrificed. Jack Shea remarks that there is a loss of visual creativity in television fare— especially in situation comedy. Instead of searching for the most effective angle or composition, the director often finds that he must merely cut from one line of dialogue to another in order to keep pace with the plot.

The ever-present figure of the executive producer militates against creativity in either the visual or auditory areas. Many producers desire "meat and potatoes" directing in order to get the assignment done as quickly and economically as possible—while retaining the special ambiance and trademarks of their series. (A fast-moving detective program may be constructed around an invincible, square-jawed hero whose hair and mannerisms are never mussed.) A director learns that he must move the production along so that everyone can collect his or her paycheck on time. Television is—undoubtedly—filled with examples of this type of production.

Directors find that they must sacrifice a careful and insightful style in favor of satisfying the producers' wants. This lack of control characterizes the present state of television directing in both the commercial and public sectors, since, with rare exceptions, producers at the Public Broadcasting Service seem to model themselves on their commercial counterparts.

On the other hand, some directors note that the technical demands of television are not dissimilar to those of features. The television screen is smaller, they argue, but composition, lighting, and editing change little as they move from television to film and back. Though one might quarrel with the simplicity of these arguments, there is more than a grain of truth in them. In fact, many of the limitations of television scripts—restrictions on numbers of characters, length of sequences, use of extemporization, and the ubiquitous character stereotypes—also characterize many films. In theater and film today there is a pronounced emphasis upon scripts calling for small casts and economical "actual location" settings, not unlike the typical television program.

The issue in this discussion, therefore, is the perseverance of directors in a medium which restricts their talent by imposing demanding pressures of time and money and a narrow range of creative forms. Most directors have learned to cope by accepting the occupation for what it is, and they try to work within it. Many others sublimate their creativity into other considerations; they learn to "get involved" with the minimal human values present in the scripts on which they must work; they search for meanings not readily apparent in the original scripts; they attempt to create interest and vitality by an artful edit or a sly expression, tucked away where the producer's inquiring eye might miss it. The successes are minimal, but they tempt the director to try to make the form more malleable.

Television—An Enticing Package Empty of Content

The director soon learns that the "commercial" in "commercial television" is the operative word. All program elements must point at the creation of noncontroversial, attention-getting formats which will suit the needs of both the seller (the networks and advertisers) and the buyer (the viewer). It is not surprising to learn that virtually all of the television directors interviewed wish to move out of their present occupation and into films, where this particular corporate sensitivity is not so pronounced.

The alternatives to working in television are not extensive, since production of film and videotape for this medium consumes the bulk of the talent and resources of the American film and videotape industry.

The values which dominate most television scripts annoy directors and writers, who find, nevertheless, that they must uphold these standards in order to sell their programs. The television audience is bombarded with a huckster mentality that stresses sales and consumption. The world of television is filled with cliff-hanging action calculated to keep a mass audience in its chairs during the commercials which follow. Seldom are humans shown as they come to grips with real issues, or with themselves as fallible creatures, trying to understand the difficult questions life poses. Instead, we are given one melodrama after another, each stressing the punishment of evil, poetic justice, and virtuous heroes and heroines who seem to have been lifted from the Victorian era.

Neither directors nor producers are insensitive to these issues. Producers tend to be educated, traveled, well-read men and women of the world. They have artistic and critical standards— often high ones. However, they have learned that television is usually a disposable part of this mercantile society. They have suppressed their sensibilities in order to survive in a highly competitive industry that rewards only one thing: public acclaim as reflected in Nielsen ratings and percentages of the viewing public.

American television in the late 1970s is characterized by ennui and hesitation. Creativity in production, direction, and writing occurs at rare intervals; television practitioners wait to see if artistic considerations of importance will ever emerge.

2
Producers, Writers, Actors, and the Government

The Producer's Power

The role of the much maligned producer must be understood before any study of the director can proceed, since this executive is not only the corporate superior of the director but also his mentor, script approver, consultant, casting chief, and the overall supervisor of any television operation. As Ivan Dixon says, "It is the producer's medium."

The producer became a necessity in the earliest years of motion picture making in the United States. Films had to be financed and sold just like any other commodity, and their merchant was the producer. His was the job in which materials, talent, and services were produced in order to create a film.

Today, in television, the producer is often a writer by training; he may have written the pilot for a series or have collaborated on an idea for a series. He is only occasionally an ex-actor or director. As with directors, he is almost invariably a male; he generally has a penchant for promoting, and may be a bit of a con artist, for without this compulsion for persuasion, the producer seldom succeeds in his chosen field.

A more or less typical profile of a producer includes an undergraduate academic degree in business or the liberal arts followed by several years' experience in talent representation. Occasionally, a producer will have a graduate degree in business or law. He is generally a native either of southern California or of New York City. His demeanor is brusque, pressed as he is by many conflicting demands upon his time. He is accustomed to making quick decisions, since he is the court of last resort in all issues involving expenditures of money. Furthermore, his background and predilections are those of an artistic or creative personality. He has definite views of what is good material, and may have established a working rationale for that evaluation. The producer works through the front office, which deals with the multiple crises of each working day.

In a series, the pre-production, production, and post-production phases overlap. While one program is being scripted, designed, and cast, another is being filmed or taped, and yet another edited, dubbed, or looped and prepared for distribution. The network production office invariably questions dialogue, characterizations, and script ideas as to their suitability for airing, to be sure that they are not offensive to viewers or advertisers, as the production office sees it.

It is apparent that this environment is not ordinarily conducive to the training and nurturing of a creative personality. Any art, diminutive or great, demands freedom, flexibility, and an atmosphere in which the artist can concentrate his energies. It is little wonder that directors are disenchanted with the ambiance of the production office.

In all fairness, the production system places demands upon the producer which bear explanation. He is neither totally commercialized nor a simple Philistine. As a product of an industry which emphasizes success, he has learned to draw those talents around him who will, most likely, bring him more acclaim and a longer tenure in his position.

In a television series, it is the producer whose ideas and reputation are being tested. Therefore, he chooses his material carefully, often repeating his last success with programs of similar content. If he was applauded for a modern, urban comedy, he will tend to select scripts replicating that theme. Conversely, if he was not successful, having perhaps a series canceled midway through a season, he will usually try a theme that mirrors another program's popularity. Imitation is the sincerest form of flattery (or the surest means of success) in American television production. In fact, it is often the only way to convince a network, sponsor, or studio head that one's services are necessary.

Directors are sensitive to the basic realities of their trade. They are seldom involved in the selection of material for television; they know that audiences are never aware of them as contributing artists. Similarly, audiences are unaware of the personalities and responsibilities of producers. Since interest and attention are the only factors which the ratings measure, these preoccupy producers more than other production workers.

No television director has the influence necessary to change a series premise, the role of a protagonist, or the visual style of a production, without the approval of a producer. Some directors began as stage actors and directors. They were used to the close collaboration of playwright, actor, and director. They are shocked to discover that key roles are often outlined and cast before their arrival on a set—at the producer's prerogative. Though lured by the promise of experimentation in a new art form, they find that the production cycle will tolerate little deviation from the patterns of past television popularity. Even the most liberal executive producers, like Norman Lear, find that the needs of the front office and the networks must override the needs of writers and directors; there is no time for luxuries like developing a cogent insight, a testy bit of dialogue, or an uncharacteristic act from a series hero.

The producer must answer to the network. The pressure which network executives apply is enormous, if subtle. A call from a network production office may contain questions about program suitability, taste, dialogue, costs, schedules, directors, producers, ratings, and competing fare on other networks. All are lightly veiled threats to the security and livelihood of producers. The entire professional career of most producers is one long search for material; cocktail parties, lunches, dinner dates, personal appearances at colleges and universities, evenings at home, and weekends with the family all can become instances in which program analysis dominates the conversation. Both the executive producer and the producer, to a lesser degree, become the foci of network, audience, and sponsor complaints; they bear the brunt of studio discontent, actors' neuroses, writers' tirades, and directors' frustrations. Television mythology has it that in one producers' office building in Los Angeles, housing approximately two hundred production suites, there occurs an average of one heart attack, nervous breakdown, or alcoholic trauma per fortnight.

The Television Writer

If the director is generally unknown and unrecognized by audiences, the writer is virtually forgotten. One has the impression at times that audiences think the words and ideas presented on t.v. spring full-blown from the mouths of actors in an extemporaneous fashion. This may be a natural corollary to the esteem with which most audiences hold the stories and characters which they see. More likely, it is merely a reflection of the potency of television's illusions.

Writers are trapped in a set of circumstances beside which those of the harried directors and producers pale. Underrated by audiences, taken for granted by actors, loved but not understood by producers, drained of their creativity by the banality of the medium in which they work, writers are often solitary workers in the production cycle.

The process by which a writer creates a complete work for television is as revealing as it is misunderstood by audiences. Seldom does a writer simply send his material cold to a producer for acceptance or rejection. Most find that they must deal directly with producers for whom they have worked in the past. Therefore, as in most aspects of the business, it becomes difficult for new talent to break into the closed circle which characterizes employment in television.

New writers must: (1) write a popular novel to which producers are attracted; (2) be accepted by a daring producer who is tired of the repetitiousness of his current stable of writing talent; or (3) have a friend who is a producer. Often, the third is far more important than any other consideration.

Once approached by a producer, the writer does not merely sit down to write a play for the screen. Ordinarily, he must acquaint himself with a series and its protagonists. Afterwards, he or she is interviewed by a producer, who asks for an oral or written "idea" for a program. If agreeable to the producer, an outline of some length is written in a period of one to three weeks. After the outline is accepted, including any changes which the producers might insist upon, a "treatment" of ten to forty pages or more is produced. The treatment serves as the complete story out of which the finished script is developed.

No script is ever complete, it seems. In one-hour melodrama and half-hour situation comedy, scripts are constantly revised as writer, director, and producers try to clarify, intensify, simplify, or make more humorous the material to be recorded. Consequently, directors and actors find that they must often film or tape sequences for which the introductory material has not been written—a process which is not conducive to highly polished performances.

In addition, the scripts which writers deliver to producers are purchased in toto by production companies. The understanding is clear that any or all of the scripted material may be altered or deleted to suit the producers. It is not uncommon for a complete script to be thrown out and a new one written by staff story editors, with only the title left intact. The writer is paid in full, but none of his words are ever recorded on film or videotape.

Immediately upon the sale of a script or an idea, writers move on to another production company with yet another idea. Since the writer earns approximately $3,500 for a one-hour script, he or she must sell ten to fifteen scripts a year to maintain a respectable income. This stress upon quantity forces most to write with a minimum of creativity and a maximum of commercial sales appeal. They carefully tailor their plots and themes to the known tastes of producers and lead actors. Their stories often become mere variations on the themes of evil, virtue rewarded, and the chase.

Directors are, generally, not pleased with the status of writers in television; obviously, neither are writers. The directors wish to have writers more in evidence when filming or taping is taking place, but they realize that the writers are off working on a new project. Writers express a desire to work more closely with directors and actors, but say they cannot take the time to polish their material, since it may cause them to lose another assignment.

The most common attempt to resolve these differences is through use of the staff, or house, writer, one who is a full-time employee of a production company. In this situation, a writer joins a group of from four to six others whose task it is to prepare all of the scripts for a series, thereby assuring a continuity of creativity and expression in the programs. In some cases—James Brooks and Allen Burns on the *Mary Tyler Moore Show*, for example—the process seems to aid all production elements. Often, however, it results in repetitious writing and the exclusion of new and different writing talent. Ironically, there is often no great improvement in the problem of writer availability, since the staff writers must create ideas and scripts on such an intensified schedule.

For a variety of reasons, therefore, writing is corrupted in television production. The writer is often rewriting or otherwise absent from a production; in fact, many actors resent his or her appearance at rehearsal because they feel the presence of anyone other than the director in a rehearsal hall has a chilling effect on their creativity. Therefore, directors often find themselves cast as writers. They alter or rewrite entirely sequences which do not seem to elicit the best performances.

Most notably in situation comedy, directors rewrite a large percentage of the script. The press of time and the lack of available writers in later production stages force this role upon them. Generally, however, directors feel that they can write well enough to fulfill the needs of the script. Often, they began as writers and find this to be a natural extension of their directorial duties.

In long-form television, the situation is decidedly different. Writers are employed for the duration of pre-production and shooting. Sometimes they are hired through the editing stage. They work in planning sessions, rehearsals, and on the set itself. Budgets are high enough to allow this extended employment. The potential outcome of a pilot is a series, so extra effort is applied to these initial programs. As a result of this longer tenure, writers like Ernest Kinoy, Loring Mandel, and James Costigan can suit their ideas to the actors far more precisely than others who are not allowed the luxury of working with actors and directors.

The scripts which result are more fully developed than series episodes. Writers assume that they will have artistic control only of pilots and long-form productions, never of episodes in a series. Therefore, most front-ranked authors refuse to write for anything other than these long-forms, once their reputation for quality is established. Ironically, television has little place for the truly superior scriptwriter; he becomes a commodity whose standards are higher than the medium which may have given him his start.

The Television Actor

All television and film actors must belong to the Screen Actors Guild in order to get employment from a production company. The simplicity of that statement belies the realities of employment in television and film; it is incredibly difficult to begin, and to maintain, a career in television acting. There are simply not enough jobs to go around.

Producers and directors will not risk assigning roles to new, unproven talent who might jeopardize the popularity of a program by inept acting or inappropriate characterization. Therefore, a relatively small coterie of actors dominates the major roles on television. Though producers extol the virtues of using new faces, they tend to rely upon old faces to animate their scripts.

A career in television acting can be confining. Actors become identified by mass audiences with certain character types. "Bad guys" tend to be cast with the same faces in program after program. Type-casting is a short cut that time-pressed producers and directors happily take to counterbalance the lack of preparation time. It also limits actors to repetitive roles.

Television directors find that their major task is often to cajole an actor into performing. Actors "cannot be forced to do what they reject," in Noam Pitlik's words. Consequently, the director is often cast as a quasi-psychologist who must placate wounded egos in order simply to get a program recorded. The main goal of creativity is subsidiary to the immediate need to get the job done.

Many directors—including film directors like Alfred Hitchcock and Otto Preminger—find that actors are not easy to deal with. "Most [actors] are illiterate," says Boris Sagal. These directors harken back to Konstantin Stanislavsky's injunction to lose one's ego in order to act. Many contemporary actors do not lose their egos.

Nielsen ratings seem to convince some actors that they have merits beyond their true thespian skills, and the director is often faced with actors who assume his interpretive role. Since these actors realize that their characters are indispensable to the series in question, they obtain contractual guarantees of their right to refuse scripts or dialogue which they deem inimical to their professional images. In short, they become miniature producers and directors. As a result, directors sometimes find that they are relegated to mere coordinators of rehearsal periods, shooting schedules, and editing tasks—all of which may be set aside by obstreperous actors. The frustrations build.

The actor in this highly competitive medium must be understood. Television rewards his or her popularity; he or she will work hard to maintain an image cultivated over many years. Directors are sometimes seen as an obstacle to career objectives.

Those who suffer most in this system are not the producers, directors, writers, or actors; they are the audiences. The emphases upon popularity, ratings, and money cause ideas to take a back seat to practical problems like those posed by unions and guilds. It is the squeaking wheel that gets oiled, as the saying goes. The public is far down on the list of priorities. No one lobbies for creativity, ingenuity, or quality in television material. If these appear—and they do, on occasion—it is by accident or pure perseverance on the part of a producer, writer, or director. There is no effective consumer movement in television, and it is unlikely that quality will improve until mass audiences exercise greater selectivity in their viewing habits.

The Government's Role

The major attempts to alter the content of television are those of various branches of the federal government. Acting through agencies such as the Interstate Commerce Commission, the Federal Trade Commission, and the Federal Communications Commisssion, Congress has attempted to aid in a struggle for more and varied programming and increased control over commercial interests. As of 1978, these attempts had failed to achieve either end.

One of the major attempts by the federal government to restrain what some deem excesses in television's depiction of violence and sex was the short-lived "family hour" plan. In essence, this was a programming plan to limit the content of early prime-time programs (7 to 9 P.M.) to material suitable for viewing by all the family. "It was ridiculous. Kids don't go to bed at 9 o'clock, nor are they denied use of their own sets," says Pat Shields. He is correct. The program failed, and official government backing for it petered out in mid-1976, after some lengthy court actions in California.

Clearly, government does have a place in the regulation of commercial broadcasting. That was the mandate of the Federal Radio Act of 1934, and it remains the concern of the Federal Communications Commission today. Difficulty comes in putting this requirement into practice. Few people deny that broadcast frequencies and geographical distribution of stations must be controlled by some impartial agency which grants licenses for the use of publicly owned air waves for commercial return.

Few agree on anything else, especially when the consideration is the content of programs. Some groups argue for a decrease in violent acts on television; others lobby for fewer commercials. Still others concern themselves with sexual acts or innuendo. Various governmental agencies ponder the alternatives and usually give up in frustration when faced with arguments about program content.

Directors find that their creative options are limited by the demands of both governmental and private agencies. "Government [in television] is a headache," says Buzz Kulik. In line with Aristotle's requirement that drama have climax and conflict, they argue against those who would censor what they see as the traditional elements of scriptwriting. The result of censoring sex and violence, say some, is dull plotting; dull plotting equals low ratings in commercial broadcasting. Something is amiss, directors cry, when audiences campaign against these elements of scripts but simultaneously watch only those programs which rank high in various ratings of violent and sexually expressive programming.

Most directors lament the paradoxes attending the government's role in commercial and public television. They resent federal intrusion into considerations of quality and content. However, they know that government control is a necessary part of the democratic process. They also know the fury of congressional investigations of content, as exemplified by the House Un-American Activities Committee hearings under Senator Joseph McCarthy in the early 1950s. Directors can offer few insights into these problems which most of America has not pondered.

3
Television Content from the Director's Point of View

The Commercial Element

Directors view television as a restrictive medium. It is as if a novelist's first concern were the inability of the novel form to contain his or her ideas. Incongruously, it seems, most directors persevere, trying to overcome the shortcomings of the medium.

It is impossible for the television production cycle to escape the pressures of the business. Economics dictate that no program may be unpopular with a large share of the audience, as determined by national and local Nielsen ratings which rank the most widely viewed thirty or forty programs. This stress upon popularity causes artistic considerations to suffer. Networks will not risk the disapproval of audiences, since there is a strong fear that this dislike may be transferred to the products being advertised.

The roots of the commercial network system go back to the days before television. Commercial radio was the natural outcome of the growth of stations in the early 1920s. Even though President Herbert Hoover stated that he could not envision the corruption of this new medium by commercial appeals, sales promotions on the air began in 1921. The federal government was puzzled and dismayed by this turn of events but found that it could do little to stop the process, since the United States had not established a federally funded radio system as had its European counterparts. Therefore, commercial radio became the mainstay of American broadcasting. Television mimicked its successful older brother when it became a national system in the late 1940s and early 1950s. Television networks also emulated the economic foundations of radio; "free" service was dependent upon the sale of the merchandise of sponsors who would pay for program production. In the early 1950s, sponsors seemed happy to support a large range of program ideas and formats. They were less interested in large audiences than they were stimulated by the idea of working with new technology and being seen as progressive and vital by the public. As long as the networks were only regional and the programs irregular (as they were in those years prior to the transcontinental coaxial cable) there was virtually no way of judging audience acceptance on a nationwide basis.

Programming in the 1950s included a large variety of dramatic programs like the *Philco Playhouse, United States Steel Hour,* and *Playhouse 90* —all of which were hungry for new playwrights and actors. Comedy prospered in the first of the nationwide clown shows, *The Texaco Star Theatre,* with Milton Berle. Red Skelton, Ernie Kovacs, and Phil Silvers introduced old stage routines to the new electronic medium and its mass audience. Melodrama was represented by westerns and detective and science fiction programs. In short, there was a large and fresh audience eager to watch a variety of presentations.

By the late 1950s and early 1960s all this had changed. Coast-to-coast networks were introduced, bringing any given program to 90 percent of the American audience simultaneously. Cable systems (CATV) brought the electronic miracle to even the most remote mountain and valley settlements. With these developments came the ratings services, organizations which could count with great accuracy the viewers watching any given program and report these totals via electronic means in virtually instantaneous fashion.

Advertisers could now know the popularity of their programs in a few hours. No guessing was needed; no experimentation with content and form was necessary. The electronic age brought certainty where little had existed before.

As a result, in the mid to late 1960s, television programming evolved into a mere repetition and imitation of the most popular formats: situation comedy, westerns, medical drama, and detective fiction. Gone were the various "playhouses" and dramatic experiments of the 1950s, the so-called Golden Age of American television. Gone also were most of the writers of these earlier programs—gone to either the stage or film. Television developed, in Fielder Cook's words, "an advertising orientation, that's all."

The new sophistication in audience measurement became paralleled by the producer's ability to imitate for the sake of selling. Television production turned to the experts in persuasion, business, and organization, who gradually took control of the networks and the major television studios. They turned away from the dreamers and the builders; those talents were no longer necessary.

The well-oiled machine of television production observed the rule of the marketplace: everything must please the buyer. No errors in judgment could excuse the loss of viewers. Testing, retesting, and close statistical analysis came to replace invention and experimentation.

In all fairness, it must be pointed out that the mass audience protested these changes very little. Maybe audiences were too diverse to express any unified position, or so overawed by the technology which had brought moving pictures into their houses that they were distracted from issues of content. Perhaps they didn't care. At any rate, the changes came rapidly.

By the late 1970s television had become so pervaded with considerations of ratings and pretested audience reactions that variety in programming had virtually disappeared. Gone are the dramatic series that began the era; gone are the insightful documentaries that exposed and analyzed corrupt, inefficient, and unfair practices by government and individuals. Gone are the mind-expanding comedies of Ernie Kovacs. The list could go on much longer.

Instead, television fare is just that, a quick, inexpensive nibble of "fun food" that doesn't quite satisfy or nourish, but catches the eye, or pleases the taste buds, for a short time. Then it is gone, to be replaced by another similar, short-lived product.

Dismaying as all this is to discriminating directors and viewers of contemporary programming, there seems to be little likelihood of rapid change. Even the experiments with "novels for television" or "mini-series" fall prey to the same mentality that pervades the bulk of commercial television. Programs are being generated from popular books like *The Money-Changers*, and *Once an Eagle*, noted for their melodramatic content, not for their artistry. These attempts to add new directions to television programming display the networks' unvarying need for the inoffensive or the voyeuristic. "It is at the point of corrupting the public air waves," says Fielder Cook. Even so, directors are eager to work on these projects, since there is an opportunity to break away from the restrictions of series programming.

Film versus Electronic Television

Television technology has also changed over the years. Until the 1960s, most programs were filmed in the same manner in which motion pictures have been produced for eighty years. That is, light-sensitive film was used to preserve the images made in studios. A large support industry developed to meet the needs of camera personnel, editors, and film processors. This technology remained relatively stable for the first half of this century.

With the invention of videotape, it became possible to record programs without using any of the traditional film production technology. Elaborate film processing became anachronistic in this new electronic environment. Film editing gave way to control rooms in which a handful of workers could perform the functions which had occupied dozens of filmmakers.

At first, independent producers used videotape to lower their costs. Norman Lear was one of the first to see the applications which could be made of this lower cost (and speedier) production methodology. By the mid-1970s, numerous production companies were employing this new approach to television.

The major studios resisted change to electronics. They had a vast investment in film and were reluctant to change to a format with which they were unfamiliar. In fact, videotape does not have the ability to store as much visual information as does film; resolution is less sharp; cameras and ancillary equipment are more bulky than with film.

However, economic arguments outweighed the esthetic and technical. As film stock and processing prices soared in the early 1970s (film being tied to the cost of silver), videotape became attractive to even the largest studios. It is, today, increasingly common to see large, electronic control room vans stationed outside of "film" stages. The changeover has begun.

As a result, those directors who have a background in video-tape production are at a premium with producers. Many who did not have this training are constant visitors on the stages of "electronic" programs, trying to absorb enough information to make themselves employable.

Traditional filming still has many advocates. Features are filmed—and will be for many years, since thousands of theaters throughout the country are equipped with film projection machinery. Film cameras are far more compact and flexible than video cameras, permitting directorial approaches which are denied by electronic equipment.

"Electronic television is limited by its present technology," as Ivan Dixon says. At present, videotape is used almost exclusively for the production of situation comedies and "daytime dramas" (soap operas) because of its lower cost. Additionally, these programs demand little in the way of visual variety, since they are dialogue-centered theatrical forms.

Current experimentation with ultrafine-scan television cameras (which record greater detail) and increased miniaturization foreshadow the end of film as the standard method of production for television. "Film is a dinosaur," says Hal Cooper. As producers and networks search for ways to lower costs and increase profits they will turn to this newer technology to meet their demands.

Television Series Content

The series idea was an outgrowth of early radio programs, mostly soap operas and detective offerings, in which a central character narrated a different story in each segment. In contemporary television, the series has evolved into a melodramatic or comic representation of unvarying sameness in which the central character is forever frozen in a posture of unerring and predictable repetition. Doctors are incapable of error. Detectives outshine the ratiocinative abilities of Sherlock Holmes. Comic leads cavort in a childlike state of benign acceptance of the world at face value. Predictability, repetition, the reward of virtue, the triumph of justice are the primary elements of these scripts. The mediocrity is overwhelming.

It is commonly argued that the poor quality of television material reflects the audience's standards, not those of producers, directors, or writers. While the audience—and its impact upon programming—will be studied later, the question of who determines television content is important. Not surprisingly, the answer is as veiled as are most other issues in the television industry.

As has been related, directors and writers lay the responsibility for program content upon producers, producers upon networks, networks upon advertisers, advertisers upon the responses of audiences. An impartial view would indicate that all share responsibility.

A more intriguing question is who benefits from the content of programs. Three groups are directly affected by program content: the audience, the networks and advertisers, and the production personnel. Millions of viewers spend hundreds of millions of hours watching television each year. Whether they are complaining or complacent, they do not turn off their sets in significant numbers (even though, in late 1977, a small drop in daytime and evening viewing hours was noted by the major ratings services). The needs of this audience are apparently being satisfied.

Networks and advertisers are, in actuality, extensions of the same system—one whose goal is product sales. They wish to bring the maximum sales impact to their product with a minimum expenditure of time and funds. Contemporary television is clearly meeting their needs, and they—like most corporations—strive to lower costs, increase efficiency, and raise dollar sales volume.

All production personnel are rewarded by this system in the creation and continuation of jobs. Producers, directors, writers, actors, and the various union personnel associated with film and television production benefit in this way. Qualitative arguments aside, the sheer volume of work generated by the commercial production system is an important economic and social force.

A reasonable answer to the question of who controls television content is that all elements contribute. Behind the system is a potent set of cultural values. We are so possessed by the need to manufacture, sell, and consume that even our arts reflect this compulsion. We try to generate audiences, in order to sell products to mass clientele; we do not put money into ballet companies for rural areas, for example. It is difficult to see the logic in blaming the networks, producers, and studios alone for values which pervade our society.

Two other forces influence the content of American television programs: government and large corporations. Both have attempted by legislative or fiscal means to alter the content of television to suit their own ends. Unlike audiences, whose impact can be charted only indirectly, through ratings, these powers act directly in their own self-interest. "Governments and corporations collude to deny quality to the American audience," says Joan Darling.

There are numerous examples of the restrictive intervention of the federal government into television: Woody Allen's *The Great American Dream Machine* on the Public Broadcasting System and *The Selling of the Pentagon* on CBS-TV are two cases in point. Federal panels condemned both programs so vociferously that subsequent ventures were withdrawn, curtailed, or modified by the broadcasters. Directors are aware of the highly sensitive audience which resides in the American Congress. They feel constrained in developing scripts and ideas.

Large corporations try to present the best images possible on the mass media. The Public Broadcasting Service is heavily indebted to the support of major businesses which help finance their programming. Do these corporations attempt to affect content? Not directly, but the programs which they underwrite are, in the main, noncontroversial and bland—perpetuating the lack of vitality in production just as effectively as if they had invested directly in commerical television.

It is the pursuit of success by producers, more than any other pressure, which determines what we see on television. In their drive to create a product pleasing to both advertisers and audiences, they repress the invention of writers, actors, and directors to a degree that is astonishing.

As a result, directors have determined the formulae for their own longevity in the business. No one wishes to lose his employment, neither the factory worker nor the television director. Similarly, few of us wish to compromise job performance by sacrificing our personal standards of integrity, industry, or craftsmanship. As it is in other occupations, so it is in television—business needs are accommodated in the creative process.

All artists wish to establish credibility with audiences, peers, and superiors. They wish to be recognized as competent craftsmen and women who deal with important issues in a manner which is consistent with content. They wish to be understood and believed. Since the influence of producers and networks is so pronounced, fledgling directors are often moved to relinquish their interpretations in favor of others'.

It is difficult to establish one's credentials as a creative director when the material is as cliché-filled and plodding as are most television programs. Directors whose ambitions lie in filmmaking are labeled as television directors for the remainder of their professional lives because they cannot break away from the double influences of content and producers.

The personalities of actors, producer, writers, and directors often cohere so effectively that they are incapable of assessing their own work as they produce it. Not surprisingly, sets of television programs often resound with the high praise and lively camaraderie of people who immensely enjoy their work. This unity—while laudable in an interpersonal sense—makes it difficult for some hard and fast decisions to prevail. As a result, directors often do not use an interpretation or camera angle which they, upon reflection, might have. The pressure of time interferes with sound directorial judgment. "We suspend our own disbelief. It appears better *now*; later we're more objective," says Noam Pitlik.

In long-form production the situation is different. Since the director has been given more authority, time, and money, better writers, and a voice in the casting, he or she finds it easier to make qualitative decisions.

For the past decade scholars and researchers of all stripes have mulled over the implications of violence on television. Not one has ever shown a causal relationship between a fictional act of violence and a long-term change in human behavior. Yet many people are opposed to glorification of violence as a means of resolving human conflict. It is not within the purview of this work to study the phenomenon; however, directors are as concerned with the issue as is the general public.

Some directors argue, as does Buzz Kulik, that violence is a part of our world, and as such is a legitimate dramatic tool; that audiences have demonstrated rather resoundingly that they will not watch programs which do not contain elements of violence; and that directors are powerless since producers and networks insist on violence as indispensable to program formats. Fielder Cook points out that "the most violent program simply doesn't compare to one hour's incidents in a Greenwich Village precinct house."

While agreeing with Kulik's observations, others, like Gene Reynolds, state that they will use all their influence to have gratuitous violence deleted. Unfortunately, most directors do not have the prestige necessary to alter script content.

For the fortunate minority of directors, a change has taken place over the past decade. Long-forms have enabled a handful of directors to deal with issues, scripts, and talent otherwise unavailable to them. These new formats have been used by some producers and networks to introduce new ideas to prime-time viewing. Using materials which are deemed inappropriate for the money-paying audiences of motion pictures, these programs have dealt with social issues of no small importance, e.g., *A Case of Rape* (rape), *Roots* (black history), and *That Certain Summer* (homosexuality).

There has arisen a rather select group of directors, producers, and writers who have established themselves as distinct from their contemporaries in television. It is to be hoped that this form of commercial television will continue to grow.

The predominant form of comedy on television is situation comedy, deriving from the conflicts found in a family or family-like setting. The popularity of this format—as exemplified by Tandem Productions' *All in the Family*—needs little explanation. Apparently, the audience takes vicarious pleasure from the adventures of characters who appear to be much like the viewers in income, dress, language, aspirations, and interests.

Producers and directors are attracted to situation comedies because of the low production costs (when compared to on-location, filmed melodramas) made possible by small casts, few sets, and actual running time recording on low-cost videotape.

Ideally, a half-hour television situation comedy can be completed in thirty minutes' stage time, a feat which is impossible in normal film production. Another difference between situation comedies and comedies or dramas done in other formats is that of the theatrical ambiance of performing a small play (about twenty to twenty-two minutes for half-hour programs) in front of a studio audience.

The Influence of the Networks

The leverage that networks can gain over producers, writers, actors, and directors is well documented in the popular press—and most of the stories are true. If we assume that the major function of commercial television is to promote sales, then the network front office's attitudes toward popularity are no surprise.

The director finds that he has three alternatives: accept directives from the networks and include them in his production; ignore the directives and try to trick the network into believing that they were followed, or quit. Since it is unlikely that the director will walk out on his livelihood, the most common alternative is the second—to sidestep the issue.

Virtually none of the directors interviewed could support the more crass suggestions of network officials. According to them, whenever they were called upon to "hype" the ratings of a program by increasing the violence or sexual overtones of a script—for no sound dramatic purpose—they would find some way of appearing to meet these requirements without actually doing so. ("Outwit them; it's often the best you can do," says John Badham.) One wonders how they can do so effectively, but most directors seem to think that it is possible. Obviously, prolonged refusal to obey the mandates of network production offices will result in the director's loss of employment.

To networks, only numbers speak with authority. Joan Darling says that television is "totally immoral," and she is basically correct. It is, however, both immoral and amoral in this context, since any fixed system of morality or ethics is of no concern to one who merely wishes to gain attention. Anything goes, unless ruled out by prior governmental dictates. Directors have no say in this process—other than to quit.

The Television Audience

The impact of audiences upon programming can be assessed by direct means (ratings) or indirect measures (attitudes of directors and producers). Each has its validity. The former is standardized, and has been discussed earlier; the latter is less easily verified but, nevertheless, is an intrinsic part of contemporary television.

Each director brings a unique background to his or her profession; therefore, it is reasonable to expect that views on audiences vary. In addition, there are different audiences.

A primary audience for directors is that composed of actual and potential employers. Learning to satisfy the needs of networks and producers is an essential skill.

Though the public does not recognize television directors as important, the men and women interviewed had definite interpretations of the wants of mass audiences. They varied in their assessments of the intellectual levels of this audience, but they could not deny its importance to their work.

The practical "audience" for the typical director is himself. Since time and production schedules will not allow most directors the luxury of actually testing audience response to a particular program (except in situation comedy—and even then, not in the crucial rehearsal stage), the director must rely upon an innate sense of theater to predict audience attitudes. It is a skill which is built up over a long period of watching and listening to audiences and productions.

Some directors argue that networks and producers underestimate audiences' abilities to grasp important or difficult concepts. Others maintain that the generally low intellectual level of any mass audience forces television to possess a higher sense of social responsibility than do films, because features cater to specialized audiences.

Although television has a variety of audiences to please—intellectual, nonintellectual, art lovers, escapists, social reformers, conservatives, etc.—the dominant force is still that of the advertiser and his extensions, the networks and the producers. If he displeases the corporation that buys commercial time, a director, writer, or producer quickly finds out which audience counts most. Displease the general public and the ratings will fall a few points; displease the producer and jobs will become scarce; displease the advertiser and employment will disappear.

4
Interviews with Directors

The Interviewing Method

The interviews in the following pages were conducted during the last quarter of 1976 and the spring of 1977 in Los Angeles, California, where 90 percent of all television programs are made. All the directors were actively engaged in production; most were interviewed over a period of two or three days while they worked on the sets of various network programs. Concurrently, the actors, writers, and producers working on the programs were also interviewed. After the programs were filmed or videotaped, each director was interviewed with an open-ended list of questions pertaining to his views of television production and direction. These interviews lasted up to two hours. After the tape-recorded materials were transcribed, rough drafts were returned to the directors for correction, in case their original words did not reflect their true perceptions. In many cases, the subjects met again with the author to clarify or expand upon specific passages or comments. In some cases, the interviews were condensed to avoid redundancy.

What follows, therefore, is not a series of off-the-cuff interviews; it is the product of a long, thoughtful process in which the ideas of these directors are recorded as faithfully as time and language will permit.

The questions range from those which are important to all directors—regardless of age, specialties, or skills—to some which reflect the preoccupations of particular directors at a given time. The unifying theme is that of commercial television production in the United States during 1976/1977. Large variations in interests and perceptions are, obviously, part and parcel of such responses.

John Badham

Badham has directed for the best-known television production units in southern California, such as Spelling-Goldberg Productions, Quinn Martin, and Universal Studios. Since 1975, he has turned to feature films, directing The Bingo Long Traveling All-Stars and Motor Kings *and* Saturday Night Fever. *Still in his thirties, Badham exemplifies the director who began with television series direction and progressed to independent motion picture work.*

Television series: Delvecchio, This Is Your FBI, The Senator, *and* The Law.

• *John Ravage:* Do you think there is a difference between the person who directs for television and the one who directs feature films?

• *John Badham*: Well, there's definitely a difference in the amount of time that you are able to spend and the amount of care you can give to any one project. Also, there's a big difference in that the producer is in control in television, and the director is in control in films. The reason for it is really fairly simple: the producer in television will conceive of a show and then be in the position of having to make twenty-six shows. He then puts a number of stories into scripts. The writers then have a tremendous time schedule to meet. The producer books directors, maybe a half-dozen directors that he likes. He will salt them through a twenty-six-week shooting period.

The director comes in when the script is done and participates in the physical preparation of the show. A lot of casting may already be done for him. The leads are already cast; the story is pretty much set and he can do a little patching, but that's about all. He's tremendously hampered by the limitations of budget and time, where he can shoot, or standing sets that already exist. His contributions are fairly minimal at that time. Additionally, there are some production companies around town that cast the show for him, pick the locations for him, everything. His function, in their eyes, is to shoot the shots on the page, to give them the coverage, to not strap them with any artsy stuff—"meat and potatoes filming." Get it done. If you are willing to go along with that process and can meet their level of quality, then they will keep you working all year around. You get a pretty good income, but you give up the right of being able to participate in the preparation of the show. You certainly give up all editing rights, even though you're contractually allowed a first cut. If you want to keep working there, you give up certain directorial rights.

For example, I encountered a situation with a segment of a series that I directed in which I shot a sequence in a very unorthodox manner. It was a scene in which a gang of hoodlums had to break up a Mom-and-Pop grocery store. Due to the speed with which we had to go at it, I knew that I couldn't film in the way the producer would like it done—which would be to take a master shot of the whole store being destroyed and then cut in individual close-ups of the toughs all over the store, destroying things. I knew that we could destroy it only once, and I only had one camera. With two cameras my problem would have been a little easier. So, I shot a master of the hoodlums coming into the store and got them in the positions from which they would start to destroy the place. I cut the camera and then did all the destruction in individual shots. One guy would dump over some cans; another would kick through the meat counter; another would turn a whole case of fruit over; another would rip open all the potato chip bags—each one isolated from the other. The theory being that, in editing, the cutting would go from this to this, to this, to this—and then back to a master shot seeing the carnage. I got a very puzzled phone call from the editing supervisor asking, "How are we supposed to put all of this together?" He said that I'd better go up and show the editor how to cut it. They led me to believe they were doing me a great favor by allowing me into the hallowed places. That's the way some producers work. They've created an assembly line and the director is just another part of process.

On the other hand, in films, the director is part of the initial idea, and he sees it all the way through to the end. He has much more latitude, much more control in every single aspect of the production. In that sense, there's a giant difference between the two media. There are also technical differences; you tend to shoot more close-ups in television, partially because you need them to get impact and partially because you don't have the time to get the performances as carefully crafted as you might like. So, you don't have master shots that run for a long period of time. If Peter Bogdanovich wants to have a five-minute scene play in one shot, he'll spend the whole day, maybe two days, getting the performance just right. He'll use as many takes as he needs. The same five-page scene done for television has to be done in half a day and you wind up with a master that kind of works; it doesn't matter if it is not as good as it can be.

The editor just starts playing ping-pong: here a reaction shot, back to here, middle of the scene, drop back to the master to remind everybody where it all is, and then bam, bam, bam, bam, back into it. Again, it's brought about by the necessities of time.

● *JR:* One director said that he saw *Lawrence of Arabia* on television and it works 98 percent as well on television as it does in the theater. It can't be both ways.

● *JB:* The people who say that have probably seen the picture in the theater and they're carrying over a lot of their experiences. *2001* was recently on the Z-channel [pay television]. There is no comparison. On television, *2001* is awful; it's just dull beyond belief. I was watching it and wanted to shake the television set. The shots were going on forever. In the theater, I was totally entranced by it, absolutely willing to go with the size of that image and be overwhelmed by it; but the smaller it gets, the more you lose.

● *JR:* One thing we're talking about is the director's control of his material. I was sitting with one director while he was making changes in the script and I had just asked him a question about control of the content. He said much the same thing that you have. Then I said, "I just saw you write dialogue. I saw you change the script." He looked up, sheepishly grinned, and said, "Yes, that's right."

● *JB:* Well, he's an unusual man; he's a man who works in both media. And he has enough of a story sense, as do several others who are also writers, to be willing to go in and to take an actor's suggestion to work with the actor's discomfort with it. Sometimes you have to do a little fudging to fit the talent you have been given. When you get the dialogue, you may find that it doesn't quite work. It's very common on Broadway for the author to sit in the theater during rehearsals, for exactly that purpose. You find out things when you get material on its feet that you never would have thought of in the confines of your office, typing away. So, you're bound to be doing a lot of on-the-set changing. If the piece is not too heavily plot oriented, if it is character oriented and you have good creative actors, you may be getting a lot of wonderful input from the actors who are just coming to grips with the material for the first time. They put their creative juices to work on it and come up with things that are absolutely wonderful. I get that all the time; I encourage actors to do that, and invariably I benefit from it. If they come up with rotten ideas, I throw them out. If I misjudge, and use the material, I can get rid of it later with the miracle of editing, right? You are foolish not to take advantage of what they can bring you.

On one program somebody came to the set one day and said, "They're very angry with you."

"Why? I'm on schedule. What's wrong?"

"You're letting the actors improvise."

I said, "Well yes, I am. First of all, if we don't like it, we can always cut it out; I've got tons of coverage here, and we're getting some terrific things."

"But you're letting them improvise; they're not saying the words on the page."

I said, "It's not that kind of scene. You don't have to say the exact words. It's a different sort of scene."

In a character, created film improvisation is a great enricher. Improvisation has its limitations and if not controlled and channeled it can make a scene muddy, long, and tedious. If well utilized, it helps the actor understand the underlying dramatic dynamics of the scene and very often will add quite creative moments.

In a very heavily plot-oriented film, however, such as Hitchcock's films, both actors and director are more constricted, because the plot is so confining. Very often it is a real house of cards that can collapse because of a wrong gesture on a piece of business. Therefore, I have found myself apologizing to the actors continually during the shooting of a remake of Clouzot's *Diabolique,* entitled *Reflection of Murder*: "Yes, I think that is a nice idea, and I think your character would do that. However, it may give away the ending. I don't think we should do it.''

●*JR:* Many directors often complain about the star-centeredness of continuing television; no matter what happens, the star must survive. Therefore, a script cannot show the growth of a character.

●*JB:* That's exactly the case. In a continuing series, people become terrified of changing anything about the main character, to have him grow, to have anything happen to him. You can't kill off the leads 'cause you know they're going to be back next week. That's one of the things that's nice about the Best-Sellers series. In twelve weeks it will be over. Leads can die, change, or grow; it's fine. However, on *Ironside,* for contrast, there were rules that Ironside could never be wrong; he could never make a misjudgment. All of the people around him, somehow, were allowed to make errors because they were just rookie cops, but Chief Ironside had to be the Solomon of the situation, even when it would have made much more interesting theater to have allowed him some vulnerability. He was protected by his producers and, maybe, by his own instincts.

●*JR:* Americans love myths, and one of our myths is that of the infallible hero. Television just perpetuates this.

●*JB:* Well, you're dealing with mentalities that are still locked in comic books with Superman heroes in various guises, even if they are antiestablishment like Baretta, or Delvecchio, who started out to be as vulnerable as we could make him. Oliansky had written a wonderfully vulnerable character and Judd Hirsch could play that vulnerability. However, the network insisted on removing that vulnerability because they felt their audience wanted a hero. Bill Sackheim, the producer of *Delvecchio,* wanted him to have flunked his bar exam, for example, but the network wasn't going to allow that.

I directed two episodes of a series called *The Senator* some years ago—my first directing job—and the first script that I did dealt with organized crime's impact upon government through the lobbyists and influence peddlers in Washington. At one point, Senator Stowe's chief legislative aide was called in front of a commission to answer some questions about possible involvement with organized crime. He got very worried about it, not because he felt that he was guilty, but he didn't know the nature of the questions. He determined to take the Fifth Amendment and announced the fact to his boss. He went in and did so. I received calls from the network and from the studio saying that one of the leading characters in our series was not allowed to take the Fifth Amendment. I argued that very shortly he would be shown to be innocent of any and all wrongdoing. He was just protecting himself in a circus-like atmosphere. They said, "Anybody who takes the Fifth Amendment is a liar and a schmuck. That's been proven by the Kefauver Commission, and if you've got something to hide you'll take the Fifth Amendment. You *cannot* direct on this show if you're going to do that."

I sat there, extremely angry, and then David Levinson, the producer, and I asked the writer to do as follows: have the legislative aide walk into Senator Stowe's office and say, "When I go to speak to the commission I'm going to have to take the Fifth Amendment." His boss, will say, "When you do that you will be fired. I can't have the taint of that on this office." The aide says that it's the Fifth Amendment we're talking about, the Constitution of the United States. It's a basic right. Senator Stowe will say, "I'm as much of a knee-jerk liberal as you can find anywhere around, but the fact is that the right of the Fifth Amendment has become so tainted that everybody will think you are covering up., Now, I know that you're in the right, and you haven't done anything. But this office can't have that cloud hanging over it. It's a rotten shame when we come to this kind of situation in our country and this becomes the way we have to deal with basic rights." The network now passed the scene, which was actually better. We came up with a more interesting examination of how people regard the Constitution.

● *JR:* You're saying that in this case the network and the studio were right?

● *JB:* No, I'm saying they expressed the country's contempt for people who exercise certain of their guaranteed rights. We said, "You are correct, people do look at it this way, and that's a rotten situation. And it's even worse if a senator of the United States is intimidated." It allowed our two lead characters to be much more vulnerable and I think we made a much stronger point than if we had just let them go in heroically and take the Fifth Amendment. I think it was a classic example of serendipity. A little one, but that, nonetheless.

•*JR:* Maybe that's the best sometimes television can hope for, little successes.

•*JB:* We spend a lot of time in television out-maneuvering and tricking network executives. One quick example: one of the shows on *The Senator* had to do with the building of a major dam on an Indian reservation. The Indians showed up at senate hearing with picket signs and said that George Washington was a liar. "George Washington gave us a treaty," they said. "We could be here as long as the grass shall grow, and the rains fall, etc. He has lied to us now."

The network looked at the script and said there was only one problem: we had to change the title; we couldn't call this show "George Washington Is a Liar." Why? Well, the network didn't want to be caught saying that the father of our country was a liar. We said, "Well, fellas, it's not that he's a liar, it's that the present administration is not honoring the old treaties." They said, "That's just the point. We can't say that about our present administration. And, we can't be casting aspersions on George Washington." So we said, "Okay, well, what would you call it? Would you like to make some suggestions?" The head of programming said, "Yes, I have the perfect idea." (He is an attorney.) He said, "I think you should call it 'George Washington Told a Lie.' " There were blank faces all around the room. We hurriedly said okay and tried to stop and think about that one. Suddenly we realized we were dealing with a lawyer. And his logic was, very simply, that if you say George Washington is a liar you're implying that everything he says is a lie. On the other hand, "George Washington Told a Lie" means that he told one lie. That's not so bad. And suddenly, that made it all right.

•*JR:* And so that's the title as aired?

•*JB:* Yes. It always amazes me that they didn't see that we were saying the same thing. We had the title we wanted. It was just that strange little turn of phrasing that made everything okay. It made one lawyer believe that people would think just as logically as had he.

•*JR:* What audience does the director of television have in mind?

• *JB:* The network and the producers are the audience they direct for. They're the ones who will employ him next week and the week after.

• *JR:* Maybe it's the only form of theater in which this happens.

• *JB:* Hopefully, he's thinking about how the eventual audience will respond to it. His success in terms of future employment depends not on the outside audience, but on the network and the producers who don't necessarily go by any audience reaction to the show. *The Law,* for example, was heavily promoted by NBC as a special event, and had terrible ratings. The audiences hated *The Law.* They could not have cared less about it. I took it to screenings in Hollywood for audience study and they were repelled by what they saw. Their responses to questionnaires that we gave out said that it was too realistic, too much like Watergate. As you know, there was no reference to big government in the program, but they were using Watergate as something symptomatic. They did not want to be told that the lawyers governing their affairs were often crooked. They didn't want to hear that. Therefore parts of it that appealed to the more sophisticated audiences went directly over the general audiences' heads. It repelled them. However, the network loved it, and the producers loved it. . . .

• *JR:* Maybe because the network was represented by lawyers?

• *JB:* Yes. And attorneys always are impressed by the program. They know that the truth was told, and that great care was taken to be accurate.

There I was having directed a show which was a critical success, and a total failure as far as the audience was concerned. However, it did wonders for my career.

• *JR:* You had the best possible kind of failure.

• *JB:* I then received more material than I could possibly read— more shows to do, more choices of things. It helped get me over into doing features. That was not my plan particularly. I was trying to do the best directing job of which I was capable.

One of the major difficulties is trying to achieve as much quality as possible in as little time as possible. It requires tremendous homework and inventiveness and great tenacity to fight against all the obstacles of budget and time. It is not a field in which creativity is particularly appreciated or admired. The thing that is more admired is the ability to get the television show done in a certain amount of time and on budget. However, what's interesting is that when the show gets all put together, no one says, "He brought it in on schedule." They simply say that the show's good or the show's poor and if you don't go *too much* over budget or *too much* over the schedule, you'll be all right; they'll keep you working. You're always walking a fine line. How much can I go over? How much can I get away with to give the extra quality that makes a show go well?

Another major challenge for a director in television: you have very little opportunity to say anything individual, on your own. You're basically a traffic cop. You stage scenes that are handed to you. A good director tries to make it as interesting as possible so that the images move with some freshness. Depending on how much time you're willing to put in and who you're working for, you can contribute tremendously to the casting and editing.

Paul Bogart

Bogart, sometimes an actor in films, has directed feature films, television specials, and television series during his career. The films include Marlowe, Halls Of Anger, Skin Game, Class of '44, *and* Mr. Ricco. *Since 1975, he has directed* All in the Family.

Television (most are long-form productions): Ages of Man, Mark Twain Tonight, The Final War of Ollie Winter, Look Homeward Angel, The Country Girl, *and* The Adams Chronicles.

• *John Ravage:* What do you think makes a television director different from other kinds of directors?

• *Paul Bogart:* Well, if you want a quick answer, that's easy. He just needs different skills, that's all. If it's a multiple camera show, he has to know how to stage to the cameras and how to shoot. Especially if you stage as fast as you do on this show [*All in the Family*], there's very little time to force the proper angles. You really have to work at it, make it all happen. And the actors are eager to oblige when possible. I'm the kind of director who hates to set up a shot and then force the actors into it. My cameras go where the actors go, as long as they don't go off the set. The real answer is that there is no difference.

• *JR:* I seem to have wandered into the midst of a developing controversy, at least a change of some proportions. That is, there are many directors who have been trained in single-camera film. Since then, however, Norman Lear has had success with sit-coms and three-camera video techniques. This is introducing shudders of fear into their lives. They realize that there is a change coming.

• *PB:* Those shudders—they also got them twenty-five years ago when television started and a whole new breed of technician was needed. The television director was born out of necessity, and I guess that the first were people who had other theater experience. They then adapted themselves to this multiple proscenium theater, which is what it is. Later, they became proficient enough to be able to concentrate on content rather than form—which is the desired result, isn't it? We've become so overwhelmed by the technical chores of chopping up the play into pictures, that it's easy for some people to think that's the greatest part of the job. It isn't. It's still important, but always more important is what the actors are doing. You don't need any more than one picture if the actors are doing it properly, if the text is right, or some crisis doesn't develop. If, for example, somebody stands up out of the frame, and you have to think what to do with the camera, that's a crisis. Current three-camera techniques are only revivals of early t.v. forms.

• *JR:* Yet, there is certainly a tradition in feature film directing of manipulating the frame, to use composition to tell the story.

• *PB:* Very often. Masters of the cinema like Orson Welles became the granddaddies of television shooting because they constructed long sequences on one camera, a technique ideally suited to television. That's why, in the dramatic shows which I always did until I came here, the longer I could sustain on one camera, the fewer were my technical burdens. Like lighting: I found that I could maintain one camera angle or move smoothly from one into the next, so that the lighting changes were not too apparent. We reduced studio noise by having fewer cameras moving around. All problems were reduced so the main thing was to act, direct, and design action so that it worked to and from the camera. You could group people in such a way that the necessary people were in view when you wanted them and were not when you didn't—if you were clever enough. If you weren't, then you had to go to cuts for the effect. That can become a major preoccupation with many directors who talk about shots all the time. I never talk about shots; I mean, shots are just elements of what you are doing, and I just think it's childish somehow, to reduce your work to shots. There are *many* other elements of the performances to be concerned with.

• *JR:* You seem to be taping plays, rather than editing filmed segments.

• *PB:* These are performances; these are not feature films, they are little performances—complete, often entirely as they were done before an audience. I hate doing pick-ups, inserts, and things like that. I have done some, but most of the time I will combine a performance before an audience with a dress rehearsal. A week ago we didn't have a performance with an audience because one of our cameramen injured himself after the dress rehearsal, and we couldn't go on. So I used the dress rehearsal, and that's what's going on the air—with a few pick-ups to fix major errors.

Now we're talking about the technique of being able to fix what you do wrong on tape or on film. What we do here is a performance that doesn't need that kind of thing, one that works *with* its flaws. I hope the flaws enhance the performance by injecting a feeling of reality into the presentation.

For years I've done dramatic specials on tape with multiple cameras, and for years before that I did them live. That was my whole background in television. There are still some dramatic shows on television. *Hallmark* is still around, and there's a great deal going on over at PBS. They're doing a lot of work. I work over there whenever I can. I love to work at the Public Broadcasting System; it's fun.

• *JR:* You are the first director who's said that to me.

• *PB:* Why?

• *JR:* In virtually every case, they use expressions like "It's a rat race," "It's messed up," etc., etc., etc.

• *PB:* That's where I go to wash Universal, Warner Brothers, and CBS out of my head.

• *JR:* Wash your mind a little bit?

• *PB:* Yes, because their objective is entirely different. They want to do things that are somewhat different, that you don't get a chance to do anywhere else. Where else does an American television director get a chance to do Ibsen, Chekhov, and Arthur Miller?

• *JR:* Or material that the commercial networks won't buy because it's not action oriented?

• *PB:* Stuff that I would never get near otherwise, I've been able to do that over there.

• *JR:* Would the commercial networks ever have done *The Adams Chronicles*?

• *PB:* No, of course not. I did the first two in that series, and I enjoyed that. Now those were taped and all the locations were real. All the dangers of live performances have been eliminated because we don't do it live anymore. You're not risking anything when you do tape these days; you can fix it as easily as you do film.

• *JR:* It surprised me to find resistance on the part of these men who are very well known directors. If people who are considered to be our leading directors have this idea of PBS, no wonder it's having its problems.

• *PB:* Their argument must be that PBS doesn't pay, and they don't. You don't get any money over there. But that's what you give up in order to do material you ordinarily can't. It's like the English actor going back to act at the Old Vic to clean his mind, playing a small role that he's always wanted to get himself into and would never get a chance to ordinarily. Well, that can happen in England; it won't happen here for the same reasons that those directors won't go to PBS.

At the *Hollywood Television Theatre* [PBS], they are most agreeable. They have limited budgets, but they will stretch themselves to give you a good production. On *Visions* they will do what they can to give you as rich a production as you could get elsewhere, and the material is original.

• *JR:* Outline your directing procedure.

• *PB:* We start by reading on Monday and then discussing the script the rest of the day; we tear it apart. First we read the following week's script, discuss it, and send the writer off with that. Then we read the one we're going to do this week, having read it the previous week; we then tear that apart again. The rest of

the day is spent around the table. The next morning the rewrites
are in and we go to work on that version. If they're all right it's a
good day, and if they're not it's not. If we're lucky we get through
the show on Tuesday, stage everything, take a crack at everything,
even the things we know are not right.

On Wednesday we go back over everything. By afternoon, about
5 o'clock, we have a run-through for the writers, the producers,
Norman—everybody. A note session follows. Afterwards, we
come down here, the script gets cleaned up and sent to mimeo. I
wait until it comes back and then block it—reduce it to pictures.
The next day, we're on camera; it's very fast. We fix the text
afterwards. On Friday, we do it again. Then we have two
performances in front of audiences. If we're lucky, we've fixed all
that's wrong.

• *JR:* I noticed that in the last few minutes, you have been adding a few words here, changing the direction there. What do
you view as the director's domain in controlling content? Here
you were, performing the job of a writer, as well as that of the
technical director.

• *PB:* Everybody writes this show. The writers write it. The
actors write it. The producers write it. Everybody throws in
things. This show doesn't belong to anybody. The characters, I
think, are the people who play them now. I think Carroll, Jean,
Rob, and Sally have *become* those characters they play. There's no
question of it. There's no way of telling them how those
characters would act in any circumstance . . . anymore than I
would tell Lawrence Olivier how to play Shakespeare.

• *JR:* You might though, wouldn't you? Isn't there a difference?

• *PB:* Matter of fact, I directed John Gielgud in *Ages of Man* on
television. I went into that by saying all I have to do with this is to
protect it. There's no way I can affect it, except to protect it. That's
my job: to be nonexistent, to help others to see the material in the
best possible way. But, as we made up the order of the program, I
would say to him, "You know, between this speech of Hamlet's
and this one of Macbeth, we have two static pieces; we need an
active one. Can you do this *Richard II* section more actively? Can
you move about more than you do?" And he'd say, "Certainly,
dear boy." There was nothing he could not do to adapt to the
necessity of the medium. He was fantastic. He would rise to

towering passions, and I would be so moved that I found it difficult to say, "Cut." He would have tears rolling down his face, and I'd say, "Cut." He'd say, "Is that all right, do you think, dear boy?" And if I said to him, "As a matter of fact, I think you shouted too much," or "You made too many faces. You should have conserved a bit more here than there," he'd say, "Well we must do it again, mustn't we?" And he'd do it again.

  • *JR:* In other words, you're saying that you did direct?

  • *PB:* Yes, but *his* performance was flawless. There are some who are merely actors who can't even take that kind of minimal direction.

I've done two or three one-man shows I loved doing. I did *Mark Twain Tonight.* It was a treat to be locked up in a rehearsal hall with Hal Holbrook for two or three weeks, as it was with Gielgud, and with Paul Scofield. I did a program of poetry readings with Scofield and his wife, and those people are one-man bands. Watching those talents at work is something one shouldn't have to get paid for.

  • *JR:* Which brings me to another question. Are you doing what you like? If you had your choice, would you do a series, a filmed show, a feature film, sit-coms?

  • *PB:* I'd love to do a good feature; everybody wants to do that. I'm not interested in doing film television—doesn't interest me; it's just cheap "B" movies about cars running around, pulling up and screeching to a stop, people running out, and stuff like that. Nor am I interested in sit-coms of any kind. This *All in the Family* is a different show. These are not sit-com actors. Carroll O'Connor is one of the best there is, as is Jean Stapleton. Nobody can do what they do. It's an education to be with them. And I've learned a lot from them in the past year and a half that I've been on the show. I've learned again, for instance, what it's like to play for an audience. I haven't had an audience to deal with for so long.

  • *JR:* The difference?

  • *PB:* Oh, marvelous. When I work in live television without an audience, dramatic or comedic, it is like a vacuum. You're trying to outguess the audience; you're trying to figure out how they're going to accept it. An audience, on the other hand, tells you a lot. This is not an ordinary sit-com, no way. Maybe I'm its audience. The first time Carroll walked through the front door, I

could hear the audience go, "Ohhhhh." Great waves of love
issuing across the lights. It was exciting. My skin crawled. To hear
them laugh at a successful thing that we planned and worked out
at great cost is very satisfying, very gratifying—and very
depressing when they don't. It's shattering, it's just shattering. It's
a wonderful thing to be gauging real audiences for a change. And
they are remarkable in the way they pull a show together.

My job, when I got on this show, was not to make it a success. It
was already a success; it had been a huge success. And it wasn't I
who was going to put it in the top ten and win all those Emmies. It
had already won all those.

• *JR:* What did do all those things? Was it Norman Lear's
writing, Carroll O'Connor's acting, or was it the mere fact that it
happened?

• *PB:* All those things, all those things. It was time, it was an
idea whose time had come, and it was Lear's bravery plus Carroll's
talent and artistry. He understands that man he plays, he really
understands him, as do Jean, Rob, and Sally. My job here was to
protect them, to bring some new juice in. It now has more
physical comedy, for instance. There's more affection, there's
more touching, there's more intimacy among them.

• *JR:* A bigot is by definition a one-dimensional human
being—what do you do to develop that?

• *PB:* Carroll conveys all sorts of unexpressed feelings for that
man. He doesn't express them in words, but we know that he feels
deeply about some things. We know that he feels deeply about his
daughter; he loves and needs his wife; he has affection for
children. There are other sides to that man. He is acting out a
narrow role that was conceived for him in his childhood. He has
no choice but to play it out.

• *JR:* How do you feel then about the conclusion that, in
essence, Archie is a prostitute; that what we have in Bunker is the
attempt to take a despicable characteristic of human nature and
make it charming, warm, delightful, and human?

• *PB:* I don't think that Carroll tries to make him delightful; I
think he tries to make him human. Carroll personally has no
sympathy with Archie Bunker, with Archie Bunker's attitude. But
as an actor he understands that man's background and what
shaped him, and he also knows that the man is not one

dimensional. He has other graces. Those are the things that he conveys so well. There are some oversimplified truths that we have to get through sometimes, but that's because a half hour is limiting and he can't get deeper into things that might reveal more about the people. I'm almost ready to take that back as I say it. Not only is a half hour or an hour limiting, it's also—at the same time—expanding, if you will.

• *JR:* What if an idea or sentiment is only worth fifteen minutes and it's got to be twenty-one?

• *PB:* Most of the time we have trouble fitting our plays into the time slots. Tonight we had to cut three and a half minutes; tomorrow we'll have to cut some more, because they expand. You know there are only about twenty-three-and-a-half, twenty-four minutes in every show, and on our show the characters make the material expand. When the characters begin to assimilate the material and digest it, it begins to fill up, and it gets bigger and bigger. The character then begins to displace the jokes; jokes are cut out readily, easily, and with no regrets, no pain. The actors constantly sacrifice jokes or will reject jokes which are inconsistent, even though they may be funny.

• *JR:* Do you think that this process of three-camera videotaping in real time, in front of an audience, will become as great a force in broadcasting as many people seem to think?

• *PB:* I don't know. I think that the film interests would like to keep a lot of that business in film. They've got a lot of people working in film, and I guess they've got to protect them. So, the amount of comedy or half-hour television on tape is minimal by comparison, and I think it might just stay that way because the business demands that it stay that way. It's out of my hands, anyway.

• *JR:* Directors often say, "No, I'm a director first. I want a good piece of material," when in actuality it ain't so.

• *PB:* Maybe that's true. I feel that the only thing I care about is making a good picture, or doing a good dramatic special on television. I came to this show to spread out, to enlarge my reach, stretch myself. And it's a good thing for me because it pays well too—I'm not going to deny that—because it's a hard grind.

I don't direct this much differently from the way I would direct *Philco Playhouse.* The differences are that there is an audience, and I have contrived as much as possible to keep the action toward the audience instead of letting it flow. We maintain a proscenium and the actors accommodate the audience much more than I would, ordinarily, ask an actor to do. They "cheat" toward the audience by instinct; they don't let themselves be hidden. Essentially, we treat each program segment as a play, and each play on its own merit—what it's about and what the objectives are with each one.

I wouldn't want to do *Starsky and Hutch*; I don't want to do *Baretta* or *Kojak*. I'm not sympathetic to that kind of material. I've done it, that kind of stuff, though.

• *JR:* Have you ever walked out on this show or any other? Have you ever said, "I won't direct it"?

• *PB:* I've tried not to allow myself to get that far. When it has happened, I've said, "No thank you. It's very nice, but it's not for me." But I have made mistakes, and I have accepted material that I thought I could fix and then found I couldn't. Then you're in trouble. Oh, I've gotten into deep trouble. I've been in feature pictures that I suddenly knew were going to be disasters. This was up front before the cameras turned—I mean that's when you know it—you really know it up front.

I used to be a good soldier and go through with it knowing I was going to lose and everybody else was going to lose. I never quit. Once I was being interviewed by a class of television students in Tennessee, and somebody said to me, "Have you ever quit?" When I said, "No, though I've gotten into some disasters," he said, "Well, why did you go through with them?" I said, "Well, you have contracts you have to go through with." And he said that if you know up front that it's going to be a disaster, wouldn't you be doing everybody a service, especially the picture itself, by letting somebody else do it, someone who might not feel the same way you do about it? Of course he was so right I was struck by my own stupidity. I once asked Maureen Stapleton if she had ever quit. She said, "Quit? It never occurred to me to quit, why?" Well, "the show must go on" is a lot of bullshit. The show does not have to go on. Certainly, it shouldn't go on if it's bad.

• *JR:* Especially if you believe whatever this is that Norman Lear has said he is doing.

•*PB:* No question about that, because you commit yourself to it—and everybody knows when it's bad. It's not like you're working with some jerk outfit that doesn't care about the quality as long as it's got enough has-been movie stars in the feature roles. But I managed to quit a show. It was a big thrill. It really was. I accepted a commitment to do a new series, to do the first episode in a new series. It looked like a very interesting project and I found myself in such a crusher between the writer-producer and the executive producer—each of whom wanted to kill the other—that I got caught in the crossfire. They each lied in my presence about what they had said to me privately concerning the other. I refused to let it stand. Suddenly I said to myself, "I can't believe that they're doing this. Each of them expects me to be silent about what they were saying and I'm the schmuck." So I said, "Wait a minute, *you're* lying and *you're* lying and *I* know it because I was present when these things happened. And I know you're trying to kill one another, and I don't want to get caught in the crossfire— so you can kill one another. I'm going home, gentlemen." I picked up my briefcase, and I left.

And I was absolutely thrilled. I got in my car in the parking lot and I screamed. I screamed with joy, sheer joy that I'd gotten out of something so oppressive. But I thought I'd never live through it. I thought, "Why have I waited so long to do this? Get out when it's wrong. Let somebody else do it who may not suffer at it the way you do."

•*JR:* What do you think is the major problem facing a director today? Government interference, the family hour, lack of material? Are there any major problems that are unique to directors?

•*PB:* Why, material, of course. It's always material. Finding something worth doing, and not just making work to pay the rent—which you have to do—and to feed yourself. It's finding material. . . . It's just finding the material.

•*JR:* That great maw that just consumes all.

•*PB:* Endlessly chews it up and spits it out. Finding something worth saying. There has to be a lot of junk on television, simply because if there were that much quality, people would be stuffed to the gills with quality, and you can't take that the same way you can't take the crap. There has to be pap; there has to be pap on television in order to while away those times when you must not be confronted with something important to deal with.

• *JR:* Contrast?

• *PB:* Right. You just have to coast for a while. I don't want to have to do that stuff, but it's got to be that way.

Hal Cooper

Cooper began his career as a child actor in the early 1930s. After his undergraduate education at the University of Michigan, he directed at the Dock Street Theatre in Charleston, South Carolina. Later, he wrote, produced, and directed numerous television programs during the 1950s and 1960s.

Television series: The Dick Van Dyke Show, Death Valley Days, I Dream of Jeannie, That Girl, I Spy, Hazel, Gidget, NYPD, My World and Welcome to It, The Courtship of Eddie's Father, Gilligan's Island, The Odd Couple, *and* Maude.

• *John Ravage:* What is the director's responsibility relative to the content of television programs?

• *Hal Cooper:* You ordinarily think of a director being separate from the content. No, not in this operation. The director, in some of the operations around town, is merely the itinerant worker who literally must take material and do his best to make it work. His input in terms of content is dismissed, and those are places where I refuse to work. It's up to an individual, depending on the amount of clout you've got. I find that kind of situation intolerable. I just won't work at that kind of place. That's what's happened to the director, as I'm sure you've discovered. That's what's happened to the director since the realization that meeting the insatiable well of television is paramount. That material has to be turned out; the most important thing you've got is that piece of paper, just to finish that which is no new thought. I'm sure that the writer became—and rightly so—the most important thing in television. Today, the writer has grown because he is the commodity you have to start with. You must start with the script, you know.

•*JR:* But sometimes it seems that all that is left of what the writer did is the title and the characters.

•*HC:* Very true, very true. But you do need the script to start with, and as that need for material has become more and more realized, the writer has become the producer. I mean, he has grown into that job more easily than in film, where the director has become the producer or the producer is a different kind of beast. The producer in film is a talent organizer more than anything else. A real producer is a guy who selects the material, perhaps selects the director to direct that material, selects the writer to adapt that material, etc. But this damn thing stresses grinding it out week after week after week after week, and there is no time to do an improvisation on a theme. To get a show you must have staff writers and story editors, and the director must be on the set. That's the only place he can work is with the people. There's homework, of course, but he's putting the show together. The writer is limited only by the twenty-four-hour span. He has an elastic kind of place in which to work in terms of time, so— while the directing is going on, while the acting is going on, while the filming is going on—the writer can be knocking out three pages and then have lunch. It's more difficult for a director who is doing a continuing series or one who is going from show to show. There is no time for him to get with the writers and really communicate about what he wants.

So there are fewer producer-directors than there are producer-writers, because the producer-writer can be in creative contact with six sets of writers. He talks their language, and he understands their needs. So that's the evolution. Now, unfortunately—as in all things in show business and any place else— talent has always been limited. So the number of guys who move into the vacuum of being the producer of a show is fairly limited. Therefore you get writers who feel that anybody who is not a writer is his natural enemy. The actor never says the words the way the author heard it in his mind's ear, as he put it down on the paper. The writer intends a shout: "Get out of here!" and the director has the actor *whisper* it. That's not the way the author envisioned it. I'm not talking about guys like Norman Lear who are very creative and understanding.

A great preponderance of writers consider directors as their natural enemies who have to be held off at arm's length to protect their words. Well, those producers say to the directors, who need the work and who don't have clout, "You do it that way and don't change a word." They don't realize that they are constipating their own words because they're not letting the creative juices from all the other production elements flow. Theater of any kind is a community effort. I mean, it's ordinary that the prop man comes up with the best idea of the day. A good director always must be a sponge and take ideas not only from those around him but from whomever . . . anybody.

• *JR:* Do you find that writers would prefer to help, to be on the set?

• *HC:* Well, this is a rehearsal problem. The rehearsal process is a kind of private place, because a good rehearsal allows everybody to be bad. The actor allows himself to be naked, exposed, as he tries to find the best way to do the material. So it has to be a kind of family setting and any time outsiders come into it, people who have not been part of the rehearsal process, there is a constricting. The rehearsal process can go on, but there's a constipating thing that happens where an actor won't try; he won't risk exposure, because an actor is the most vulnerable of all of us. It's *him*—it's his face. He's out there and if the public hates or likes anything, they always hate the actor first. You know, they don't say he had bad dialogue or he had bad direction: "He stunk."

So the actor's most vulnerable. Now, when you're doing a series, if you make the writers part of that family, so that they become part of the woodwork—it's okay. I find that, by and large, writers get bored with rehearsals because it is a repetitive process. It's over and over, quite often the same material, trying to find a way to make it better. Or, certain rehearsals are a memorizing process where the actor says, "I'd like to try this without my script. Feed me the lines." They're missing lines as they try that or saying the wrong words, and have to be corrected. After a while it gets to be frustrating for the writers. So I find that writers who stop in and visit stay for five or ten minutes and leave. Because they have work to do. Sure, they would like to feel free to be there.

• *JR:* I think that's an important point. They'd like to feel free to be there even though they probably wouldn't take up the opportunity.

•*HC:* But, that is not an easy thing, as I pointed out. It takes nurturing. It takes working on, because an actor is a delicate mechanism, as I said, naked, and a writer can say, "Why don't you just *say* those words?" Nothing will make an actor more uptight than that because it's an oversimplification of what their creative input is. You know, they each have their own problems, and we do quite often in rehearsal run into problems that I can't solve. I get on the phone and say, "Charlie, Artie, come on down and take a look. I want you to look at something." They come down and we present the problem. They go off and fix it with the writing we need. It happens all the time. And that's the kind of "being invited" that I think writers want.

•*JR:* What is a television director? What makes him different from a film director or a theatrical director?

•*HC:* Of course he's different—depending on what he's directing. Obviously, a news or sports director is different from a motion picture director because he's doing an entirely different thing. He's covering a different kind of face, not of his own creation, and attempting to capture it. He does it creatively because his selection is creative. But it is creative in a different sense.

Television directing is different in various ways. If the director is working on film, of course, like the Mary Tyler Moore operation, he has a certain kind of restriction. First of all, he's doing it in front of an audience, so he has to have more the approach of the theater director. He rehearses for a week and then does the play for an audience. He has the disadvantage of not having tryouts, previews, testing of the material in terms of laughs and jokes and what not—so he has to go on with little more than his own gut instinct.

•*JR:* You videotape programs here at Tandem Productions. Why not use film, as other situation comedy shows do?

•*HC:* The film camera is really a dinosaur; it's an outmoded vehicle. You have a center camera which shoots the cover, and two cameras at the side which film the close-ups. Quite obviously, that terribly restricts your ability to photograph it the way you would conceive it if there were no audience and if you had limitless use of your camera and angles, as in a feature film. Your master is by and large always in the center of the stage, and your close-up cameras are at the sides. Every once in a while, if you really fight for it, they'll give you a zoom so you have some flexibility of size on the side camera. It becomes very complicated because you have a dolly pusher, you have a man racking focus, and you have a man operating the camera itself. Now you have to mark the actors very carefully, because every place the actors land, the camera must be in focus. So the distance between the lens and the actor at that given point has to be measured in rehearsal and preplanned. If the actor misses his mark, if he goes closer to the camera or further away from the camera at a given point on a line, three people have to make the adjustment with the actor—and they get very good at it. In other words, they watch the actor's feet and they see he's missing it by six inches. An instant decision has to be made whether the dolly man is going to move six inches closer off his mark or whether the focus guy is going to rack focus a little bit. But nobody can really see what they're getting.

The same camera, the same situation in television taping. The picture is constantly being fed to the cameraman. He runs his own camera; he moves his own camera; he operates his own focus, and he's got a zoom lens. So if the actors spread a little too far apart by missing their marks, he can gradually loosen his shot. You are restricted only by approximately 180 degrees of coverage as opposed to the 360 degrees of single-camera film. You trade that off for the input and the adrenalin and the juice you get from a live audience responding to material. You can't measure that. You lose some perfection of performance in front of an audience, but you gain an awful lot. You gain a kind of excitement and adrenalin that is very hard to duplicate in single-camera filming.

• *JR:* Is this the format that you prefer to work in?

• *HC:* Strangely enough, no. The director really has the most control with the single camera. The director's tested more in feature film comedy. He has to be righter more often.

• *JR:* Describe your taping practices here at *Maude.*

• *HC:* We do a run-through with ourselves and some people from the office staff, so we get the feeling of it. Then we do a show in front of the audience at 5:30, and that tells us a tremendous amount. We find all the places we fell on our face. And because we're surrounded by such good talent, invariably somebody recognizes why. If it's not me, it's the actor or it's the producer, or it's my co-exec producer, or it's Norman who says, "Here's why that didn't work," or "We need a new joke here." Between 5:30 and 8 we change it. We make those corrections. So we've had the input of the preview audience and we've had the sustenance of the adrenalin of audience reaction which puts the actors on their kind of high. That's what feeds the actor.

● *JR:* Those of us who teach, talk about, and write about film tend to think of feature film as the way the director uses his frame to tell his story, through juxtaposition, through angle, through lighting, that kind of thing. It seems that television directors seldom use any such things. They don't use composition to make a statement. They use a line of dialogue to make a statement.

● *HC:* That's true. I think that's very true, and that's because long ago someone recognized what television in the home is *not*. People are ironing, or they're walking around, they're *not* in a seat in a darkened auditorium where their focus is absolutely forced to the stage, the screen, whatever. As a result, you have to use a little radio. One has to use dialogue. It just is so. To not recognize it is to be naive.

● *JR:* To be unsuccessful as a director?

● *HC:* So you do need the verbal. Now I don't ignore the composition. I pay a great deal of attention to composition, but it can't stand by itself to sell the story. It is supportive only.

● *JR:* It seems to me that it would be tough to compose a bright, flatly lighted sequence such as you get in MTM productions and TAT productions and do much with composition, because the thing that's twenty feet upstage is as bright as the thing that's right next to you.

● *HC:* You do have opportunities. I mean, we've had nighttime bedroom scenes and dark, where you do get a little mood lighting.

Next week I'm doing a show based on *The Desperate Hours,* with Maude and Vivian trapped in their own house. It's comedy, but it'll have some spookiness in it. It'll have those elements in it and they will definitely support the play, but you can't do it without "What was that noise I heard?" or you need . . .

● *JR:* A hyped-up noise.

● *HC:* Yes. But you can't rely on that.

●*JR:* Subtlety of either the visual or aural kind is generally missing from most television programs, comedy or drama.

●*HC:* That's right.

●*JR:* Thirty seconds of silence in the theater is crushing; in television it's not.

●*HC:* That's right.

●*JR:* What do you look upon as your best work and why do you think of it as such?

●*HC:* Well, I think the best work that I've done I'm doing now. Or maybe that's my nature to think that. Norman Lear builds an atmosphere that allows creative people to work and let their juices flow. You feel absolutely free here to do something badly. That's the freest you can be, because it allows you to stretch; it allows you to try things. Norman does that. Some shows on *Maude* are just goddamned good pieces of theater. "The Analyst" strikes me as one on which we worked so hard, and it was rewarding. On another program, "Walter's Drinking Problem," we dealt with a most serious issue. Alcoholism is not funny.

●*JR:* Why is television limited to minor attempts to answer serious social problems? Is it merely that any such drama is unpopular with a mass audience?

●*HC:* It certainly has been and it's because the director in film is more the *auteur.* He has more control. He's more being tested. You can do more adult things in the theater for an audience that pays to get in than you can for something you put on the air for free. Therefore we must be discriminating. This means that we censor—knowingly or not. We censor to a certain extent what we do on television. Someday *this* may change. Norman Lear has been more a leader in breaking out of this old form and recognizing what is going on in everybody's home. Until Norman did *All in the Family, Father Knows Best* was the picture of "reality" of the family on television. That family you saw on television was nothing like your family or the family next door or your relatives' families. They didn't speak in the same language. Since *All in the Family,* television has caught up with what is really happening in everyday life and, therefore, become a better reflection of what's going on.

●*JR:* Are there important differences in approaches which you take to film or television programs which you direct?

•*HC:* Film is a misnomer. It's theatrical release that you're talking about, theatrical viewing, as opposed to home viewing. I think the way in which that package is put in front of the theater audience is terribly unimportant. You can do the same thing on film, electronically, with laser beams, beamed off a satellite into a theater—as long as the creator, the author, the director did this thing, captured it. However he captured it, he is showing it for the approval of an audience that paid to see it, that's really what they're talking about. They're talking about composition. Now you can have composition in anything, whether it's film or television.

•*JR:* Compared to theatrical and film directors, how do you direct for television?

•*HC:* More carefully than one does for single-camera film, because there you can always cut, explain what you want that wasn't gotten, and go again. You don't have that luxury here. And more carefully than in theater because in theater only four hundred people see the show at a time. You can fix what's wrong with it for the next six hundred people who will see the show tomorrow. Here everything must be Broadway opening night without a previous audience, a real audience, and you don't get another crack. You get two shots at two audiences. So those four hundred people in the studio have to be reflective of the millions who are going to see it. Because of that, we take a mostly theatrical approach.

We read a script two weeks in advance. On Wednesday morning we read the show we're going to do two weeks from now. I have been in; I may or may not have seen this final piece of paper, but I've been in on the planning of it, and read a draft, and given my notes, and had rap sessions with the writers and the producer in charge of writing. We read that script and then we talk about it, from beginning to end: things we like about it, things we don't like about it, things that work, things that don't work. The writers take note of this, and put things aside to be worked on.

We then read around the table, now the script that we had read a week prior. We usually have a pretty good time with it because the actors are being an audience as well. We indulge ourselves, you know, and laugh where we think it's funny. We then go through the script a second time and stop when an actor has a problem with a line, or a joke doesn't seem quite right, or a point could be made more clearly. We fix those things or, if they're complex, we say, "Okay, writers need to work on that."

After the second time through, everybody departs but the director and the actors. Then we put it on its feet, and we block the show, usually on Wednesday. We walk through the whole play without any props and see what problems we have with physical business and what extra props are needed. On Wednesday night I do off-line editing; I edit the show that we finished Tuesday night, and I spend the evening after I dismiss the actors at 5:30. I'm there from six to midnight or one o'clock, editing the last show. Usually it's a six- to eight-hour session. Sometimes much less. Using two shows—the best of both shows. All of that is put on a cassette. Then we edit that show. I screen it and the writers look at it. Thursday morning we come in and we rehearse all day, from 9:30. Now it's a play; it's just a play. We rehearse from 9:30 till six o'clock at night, with an hour break for lunch.

● *JR:* By "rehearsing," you mean line interpretations, character?

● *HC:* Everything. Everything. An absolute play rehearsal. If you know a theater rehearsal, that's what it is. It's closer to a summer stock rehearsal, because you don't take time, as you would in the theater, to sit down and philosophically analyze. That's not necessary anymore because now I'm doing the twenty-third or twenty-fourth act of the same play. The same people are playing the same parts; there are no surprises in character, or at least very few. We can invent some. But they know who they are, and they know how they respond to a given situation. So we don't need that part of theater. Timing, interpretation, where to pick up the pace or slow it down, everything you do in the theater we rehearse in our play. Thursday night, by the way, I have probably attempted to "sweeten" the blending of the two shows from the week previous. Friday we come in, and at 3 o'clock we redo the play for the writers and producers, with props, with everything. If I feel the cast is shaky in lines I'll stop rehearsal, sit down at the table and just run words with them so we get the words out of the way. You can't begin to perform until the words are almost second nature, you know. Now all the time, I have been mentally staging this play;

I've been mentally photographing it, thinking of all the movements. I will stop in rehearsal and say when to deliver a line, for example, to an actor.

After Friday at 3 o'clock we know the timing of the play. A watch has been run on it; we know whether we're long, whether we're short—most of the time we're long. The invention of business tends to spread a little bit, and we find out what we have to cut. So we'll make cuts around the table. On Friday we finish around the table, and send the actors home. Then we make whatever changes have to be made. Maybe there have to be some rewrites of something that's not clear. We get together with the writers and they fix what has to be fixed. The whole fresh script is sent out Saturday morning to everybody involved, with all the corrections that have been made. Sometimes Saturday or Sunday, depending on what I'm going to do with my weekend, I take about eight hours to mark every shot in the script. When I do that I'm reviewing. This is a major difference between television directors and a film director; I must do my basic editing before I shoot the show. The film director has the master and the close-up and all the coverage, and he can do his editing leisurely after the show. He's made sure that he's got all the elements he needs for that piece of work. I have to make sure of that beforehand, although I do have the option of making minor adjustments. By and large, in order to get the audience to respond, I must be on a particular face at the precise moment because the audience that comes to see the show, strangely enough, only glances at the actors. They usually watch the studio monitors. That's their comfort.

● *JR:* It's something that philosophers ought to deal with: a basic change that television has made in how America watches things.

● *HC:* McLuhan is right, you know. Anyhow, after I've marked my script on the weekend, I send a messenger with my script to my a.d.'s [assistant director's] house. He copies my script for the technical director and makes camera cards for each of the cameramen; all their shots are listed numerically. On Monday morning we come in and run it dry in the set. We've rehearsed in the rehearsal hall, not in the set. Unlike the film operations that have a stage of their own, these stages turn over. That's an economic thing; the stages serve two or three shows.

• *JR:* They actually tear down? They don't have a permanent set, for instance, for Maude's livingroom?

• *HC:* Struck and reset because they get three shows out of that same hunk of real estate. They do a show which works Monday and Tuesday; they do a show which works Tuesday and Wednesday. We rehearse on Monday with cameras, and on Tuesday we do our show. Yesterday we rehearsed this show on camera, blocked it all out, rehearsed it all day long on camera, and set every shot. In the morning we did a dry run-through for the actors, with all the props, costumes, and everything. Then I brought the cameramen at 11 o'clock. The cameramen came in with their shot sheets. They stood and watched where the actors would be for each of their shots, and they saw where they have to be and how fast they have to move from one position to the other.

Then I go down to the control room and we rehearse. We do it over and over until we get it all right—each successive shot—and then we run that scene on camera. We do that until about 4 o'clock; at 4 we do a run-through with costumes and with props. We do a run-through for producers, writers, and the people around, after which we have notes, which we had last night. We knock off about 5:30 or 6. Today we come in, and at 2 o'clock I'm due down there. The actors are in now, and they are running lines around the table right now.

The process is such a comfortable one now that when there is a show that hasn't had that many changes, I don't have to be present at that. It's for their review, and it's better if I'm not there, unless there've been some changes I want to talk to them about. At 2:30 we will go on camera and run through the show at a leisurely pace to make sure everything is set. Then we will have a dress rehearsal for ourselves, somewhere around 3:30 or 4, after which there will be notes to the actors on the basis of that dress rehearsal. At 5:30 an audience is there; we do a show. Afterwards we have a meal break with notes on that show, whatever the audience taught us, or didn't teach us. Sometimes we're bull-headed and say, "That audience didn't get this line. I think it was the audience. They didn't seem to get the smarter jokes; they got the pies in the face, you know, so I have faith in this line and I think it will work."

• *JR:* It really is like repertory.

●*HC:* If all goes well, I will now have recorded both my shows on half-inch tape. If there was a fluff on a given line in the second show we'll go back, run the half-inch after the show is over and look at it on the previous show. If it's good on the previous show, I'll run the second show down to that point and look at the two and see if I can get from the first show with an edit to the second show, or vice versa. If it's okay we go on. Other times there will be three and four pick-ups, five pick-ups. Maybe it's a line; maybe it's a sequence of two or three lines; maybe it's a rewrite—those smart jokes still didn't work and we found out why they didn't.

We run through four weeks, and then we usually take a week off. We run through another four weeks and we take two weeks off.

●*JR:* What do you see as the major problems facing television as far as directors are concerned?

●*HC:* There are major problems. The major problems revolve around the two kinds of television being made. One is electronic television, which I am currently in, and the other is film television, which I have been in. The problems are different in each. The major problem for the director is to have his voice heard, and to have his talent respected. By respected I don't mean appreciated—*respected.* I stress that all the time.

By and large you must respect the fact that the writer tried to do the best piece of work that he was capable of at that moment, and maybe that joke that you don't like or that line of dialogue that seems terrible may be the result of his having paced the room for four hours before he was able to come up with it. Maybe he's not pleased with it either, but there was creative effort that went into it. I think that mutuality of respect is very important. But the television director's basic problem is that he has evolved into an itinerant worker.

●*JR:* Permanent itinerants?

●*HC:* That's right. They go and pick their grapes; they do one *Kojak* and two *Baretta*s—one of these, one of those—and, as a consequence, they're a Johnny-come-lately, until they establish the rapport and do enough shows to become familiar with all the elements. Everybody on the set is more familiar with the work than is the director. That makes the director not able to do the best directorial job. He has to farm out too much. He has to rely too much on other people's knowledge, which—if he had it—might alter his creativity and cause him to do his job better.

• *JR:* I got the idea that the a.d. is much more important, creatively, to that film.

• *HC:* Well, he's important—not creatively—I object to that word creatively. He's important mechanically. He's the only member of the Directors' Guild who follows a series through. But his is a different function. He's a guy who keeps all the elements in line; he's not the man who says, "This shot should be shot on the crane looking down," or so and so. That is not his function. If it is, then you really have nobody who is director; you have a mechanic who comes in and says, "Where do I shoot this shot? You'll be up there, that's your angle, and you'll shoot and he'll come in." A guy who just says "Roll 'em." He's hardly anything. So the director is always put in the position of having to fight to have his input. I don't even want to give it the word creativity. You don't need high-falutin' words to explain his job. He sees in his mind's eye what he would like a picture to be. The elements are against him, and it's mostly because of the moving about that he has to do.

• *JR:* What's the solution?

• *HC:* Well, there are various solutions. Sheldon Leonard solved it a long time ago when he did *I Spy.* He had two directors, and he signed them for the season to alternate (they did every other show) so that they were always in contact with the creative elements. They were able to function that way. That's one way to solve it. Pay them enough money so that they will not stray to other directing jobs when they're not directing. So what you have to do is get two guys, pay them enough over scale so that the week they're not shooting they are happy to do preparation for the following week.

• *JR:* Does that cut down on the number of directors practicing?

• *HC:* I wouldn't think so, no. The same number of shows have to be done, but it is more expensive. Unfortunately, the production companies and the networks want programs for the cheapest dollar possible. Nobody can ever fight that. So it's a continuing process, a continuing struggle. You always have that in a feature film or anything. A director is against the front office, he wants not to waste money, he wants to spend money properly and to get the best product that he can. It doesn't always show up on the copy sheets that way. If you want to hire the actors two weeks in advance of shooting a feature film, to rehearse, that looks like a bigger expense. It looks like an expensive project. Actually it may save a tremendous amount of time in shooting, because you don't have as many retakes; people know what they're about to do. They have an idea. They've been rehearsed in the scene. You get more in the can quickly; but "up front" in the budget it looks like a big thing, and the front office won't buy it.

•*JR:* When I asked Steve Spielberg the same question, he said, "Time and money. Time and money."

•*HC:* He's very right. He's absolutely accurate. The other problem for the director in television, currently, is the number of writers who are producers who consider the director to be his enemy. I use the word "number" very carefully, because there are many writer-producers who recognize the importance of directors. Norman Lear is the prime example. Norman is basically a writer. He operates from a writer's gut, but there are so many places that the directors suffer because of that feeling of protectiveness of the written word that writers naturally have. There are many people in the business—I've heard it said of Grant Tinker, I've heard it said of Gene Reynolds—there are people who have an ability to recognize writing and directing talent in other people.

•*JR:* Are there any other comments about direction that come to you that seem to be significant that somehow or other haven't been mulled over?

•*HC:* When you go into a control room for the first time, it can tend to be overpowering. How the hell do you do that? There are four pictures going at once, and how do you snap your finger and get the right picture at the right time and plan it so it comes out properly? The basic thing that a director has to do is to be able to read a script, to read it and see that movie in his head, in his mind's eye. You read a script. Those people are moving for you; you see them close; you see them far away; you see them in a particular room; you see them moving. If you just focus on that, and if you can see the movie you would like to make out of that script, if you just tune into that movie that you see in your head, your vision will be unique. Yours is what you have to contribute. All you have to do is learn how to transform that onto the screen. That's an oversimplification, but it's a very basic starting point. Too many people look at the monster, the device, and they forget entirely what they started from when they read the script. They make everything a compromise to the mechanics. "The camera, camera two, can't get from his close-up to that two shot. Okay, so I'll make them both two shots." That's not what you saw in your mind's eye. You saw a close-up in your mind's eye when you read that script. That's how you saw it. That's yours. Nobody can do that but you. What you have to do is find out how to get that close-up.

Joan Darling

Darling is a relative newcomer to commercial television. Her background is that of an actress, having appeared in The Troublemaker, The President's Analyst, *and* Kansas City Bomber.

Television series: The Mary Tyler Moore Show; Three To Get Ready; M*A*S*H; Mary Hartman, Mary Hartman; Phyllis; Rhoda; *and* Doc.

● *John Ravage:* Is there a distinct animal called the "television director?"

● *Joan Darling:* Yes. First of all, I'm a really good one to talk about that because my experience has been so peculiar. Television came to me to be a director. I had no interest in directing. Norman Lear came to me with the *Mary Hartman* pilots. My connection to a director was an unconscious connection. I've had hundreds of experiences in television as an actress and had no awareness of the director's function. As an actress, I only knew that I had to defend myself from the directors who came through week after week after week. With rare exceptions, most of the time a television actor will learn by habit to defend himself from the director and take care of himself.

When I got the *Mary Hartman* pilot scripts—since I wasn't ambitious to be a director, and since I was from New York and the theater—I thought the director was the boss. Sort of an assumption on my part. So I went into Norman's shop and said to him, "Here is my concept of *Mary Hartman*, what I think these two scripts are. Oh damn, it's the way media presents America, the way America presents America to America." That was the basic concept, one continuous promise of joy if you continue to brush your teeth and use the right underarm roll-on, go to church—all things that we are promised to make us live happily ever after. And *Mary Hartman*, of course, is the satire of what happens to people trying to live that way. And if Norman liked that idea then I would be willing to try directing. Norman said he loved it, and that was terrific. So then I started casting. Norman suggested Louise Lasser for the lead; I just loved her, and knew her and thought it was a brilliant idea.

And then I started interviewing other people. At one point I heard they had made an offer to an actress. I called on the phone and said, "Is this true that you've already made an offer to an actress that I haven't met?" And they said, "Oh, well, Norman thought it was a good idea." So I said, "Well, there's no point in hiring me. I'm not a director, no ambitions toward it. My specialty is dealing with actors. It seems silly to have me direct people that you merely *hand* to me." He said, "Of course, you're absolutely right. We're just used to doing it differently here."

My point was should you go with an unknown director as a technician if you're hiring one who is supposed to do magic with actors? At least you should let that person cast. There was nobody cast in that show that both Norman and I didn't love 100 percent. If I loved somebody 100 percent and he didn't, we went on further 'til we found somebody. If he loved somebody 100 percent and I didn't, we went on further. So I had the control of the casting in that show. I didn't answer to a network; that was also peculiar. Norman was my collaborator. That was Norman's choice, and unbelievably generous in hindsight. It was just staggering, the power that he allowed me to have. I got the scripts. He went away on a vacation, and I got on the floor as I did many times in improvisational theater when a scene wouldn't work. We set up the actors, and I sat on the floor and we did the rewrites; we made it work. At the end of the week he looked at it and loved it. Then I caught a shock because he started talking to my actors over my head. "Wait a minute," I thought. "When did you start talking to actors? What is this?" Well, it is his store. But I am the director. I went through all that stuff, but he was very generous. He gave me the suggestions—they were all terrific suggestions—and he really functioned as a producer would function. Then he left me alone to shoot the show. It never dawned on me that the final questions of taste weren't mine. When I got done with the shooting, Norman said to me, "You go do your first cut 'cause that is where you're going to learn about directing, so go and do your first cut." Again I had no idea how generous, in television, that is.

So I did the first cut with Al Burton helping and teaching me . . . then the second cut. Then Norman came in and looked at the cut, we discussed it and, basically, the cut that finally went on the air was mine. Well, I thought *that* was the job. Then I went over to Mary Tyler Moore. There the producer/writer is the creative head. He is the *auteur* instead of the director. I find television directing very unartistic because what's interesting to me—if I'm not going to be an actress—is to paint with my eye. If I love the material, then I go ahead and paint a picture of it. I feel free to change a line here or do other things if something doesn't work.

T.v. producers, Norman excepted, Gene Reynolds of *M*A*S*H* excepted, seem to want me as a director to work my magic, but they take away all my tools with which I do the magic. And when I make an artistic point there's no question that all I can do is offer them my best judgment. They win. That's their right, their prerogative. They are the creators.

In something like *Rich Man, Poor Man*, where they have a program going for over twenty-six weeks, I can only service the story. You have to buy the cast, sight unseen. One of the things that's interesting to me as a director is to go into situations where there aren't good actors and to have the dual problem of teaching them to act and to direct the material at the same time. What happens is that I am very successful at this. The actors like me because they get much more help than they ordinarily do.

● *JR:* Because you're a secure actor?

● *JD:* Well, that's my job as a director. No, that is my job. I've got somebody who is insecure; it's my job to seduce him to be comfortable 'cause he does better work if he's comfortable. And the actors seem to be consistent in my work. People say, "Jesus, the performances were so good in that particular episode." Part of it is an intangible thing that the actors experience that I create very consciously. *M*A*S*H* was a terrific experience because I was allowed in as a collaborator.

● *JR:* Nonetheless, the one segment you directed was a "woman's" show. It's too bad you couldn't have directed a show about a bunch of guys who had masturbation problems.

● *JD:* Right. However, the first one I did at MTM was about a poker game.

● *JR:* What differentiates a television director from a motion picture director?

● *JD:* Power! Power, power, power! A television director generally has to serve the producer/writer who is the king in television, and/or the network. He is simply a functionary, carrying out other people's ideas most of the time. At *best* he can only *participate* in it. A film director has much more of an opportunity to be an *auteur*. Ultimately, most film directors get to do the film that *they* want to make, with little interference—lots of advice, but little interference. In television—all interference and not much advice.

Money? Much better in features—much less certain. You can actually make a better living directing television because of the certainty of jobs. You make a lot more per job for a movie, but a movie takes much longer to do.

Talent, acting and writing: I certainly think writing talent is a tremendous help to a movie director, because he does have an opportunity to function as an *auteur*; whereas in television you are not allowed to write anything. In the movies you are participating in the development of the script, usually. Also, television takes on smaller stories and movies take on larger stories, so your internal design can be much larger in a movie.

● *JR:* What formats do you prefer and why?

● *JD:* Movies first. Television movies second, but I haven't done one yet. Series segments are difficult because you have less and less power in relationship to the conceptualization and execution.

Specials? Specials on PBS, I thought, were going to be terrific, but I found them even *more* concerned about offending people and more frightened to deal in large, complicated concepts than the networks.

● *JR:* Who are the best television directors? Why?

● *JD:* I can just name people who I think are wonderful. Gene Reynolds: terrific comedy director, sensational. Let's see, who else? I think Buzz Kulik, who devotes himself to television a lot, is brilliant. I think Lamont Johnson's television work has been excellent. Jay Sandrich? I have great admiration for his contribution to the concept of the *Mary Tyler Moore Show*, and I think he is a very, very talented man. Dan Petrie, of course.

● *JR:* Which are your best productions? Why and how did you achieve them?

● *JD:* *Mary Hartman, Mary Hartman,* because I had the kind of scope and freedom that you have in film, and it was a subject that I was absolutely fascinated by. I was able to develop myself in developing the material, and I was able to say something that I always wanted to say.

I like my *Mary Tyler Moore,* "Chuckles Bites the Dust"; that was nominated for an Emmy because it was about a very difficult subject. Trying to make death funny and working with that company was such a pleasure. The performances and the people were so good. And I loved the *M*A*S*H* I did this year. I thought my work was excellent. I thought the company of actors were superb and Gene Reynolds, again, very, very warm and very generous in terms of what I was allowed to bring to the piece.

● *JR:* What should, in a hypothetical sense, a director have to say about content?

● *JD:* In television it's impractical. It's the way it's set up now. It's impractical for the director to have any relationship to the content; however, I would think in long-form television or in a show like *Mary Hartman,* the director should be a guiding force in the creation of the concept. He or she should stay around long enough, and have enough freedom, to develop the concept in terms of supervising writing and casting, actually directing the segments until it's developed and can run by itself.

● *JR:* How do you direct the actors, the camera, whatever?

● *JD:* Well, in television I start with the actors and the script. I start with what I want to say with the script offered me, and then I don't tell the actors to say it. I wait and see what the actors want to say, and then I start shaping it all toward the philosophical statement behind the work. I won't know until I actually get on the set how much of the preplanning I will use, because I want to take a look at what the actors have to offer me dramatically.

● *JR:* Do you work with the talent in a theatrical fashion?

● *JD:* Well, in a film there are so many skilled people around that I try to get everybody to give me as much information as they have. I also want them to participate in the project so that they have some sense of reward too. In television, most of the time I'm a functionary of somebody else. But, again, my philosophy of directing is to make a happy family in which everybody participates in the making of the baby, if for no other reason than I think the babies are better. Above and beyond that, if you get run over by a truck the day after the movie is released, at least you had a nice experience shooting it.

● *JR:* Do you have any trademarks? Camera movements, shots, angles, positions, set design, any idiosyncrasies?

● *JD:* I'm still too much of a novice in terms of camera movements, angles, shot positions, and set design to have any idea what my trademarks will be, although I think the trademarks should be dictated by the material, not by the director. In other words, each piece of material demands a different style if you really are being true to the material. In t.v. I used a three-camera set-up. In *Mary Hartman,* I used dusty colors, dusty lighting, very soft and beautiful.

● *JR:* Can you identify others by such measures? Who and how?

● *JD:* Howard Hawks for instance, he's an *auteur* even though his pictures were always very, very simple. Tell the story, tell the story, that's all he cared about, and that's what I like. Spielberg's work is distinguished by *incredibly* sophisticated comprehension of all the possibilities of camera work, and he also seems to fit the style of the picture. I'm always impressed with John Schlesinger's work in terms of the incredible pace and action. It's packed full of life. His pictures are just packed with life, whether you like them or not. Mike Nichols' intelligence and point of view blow me away. He also has a sophisticated knowledge of pacing in a picture. Arthur Penn is fantastic, perhaps my favorite. Even his failures fascinate me because of the philosophy behind them.

● *JR:* Why are there so few directors who work in both television and theatrical release motion pictures?

● *JD:* I would guess, once you get into theatrical release motion pictures, it's such a bigger, better ball game, that, if you can help it, you don't go back to television. Television just is a much smaller scope for the director. He just doesn't get to do as much.

•*JR:* Is directing in front of an audience different than films?

•*JD:* Yes, because, if you are talking about plays, you lose control over the performance and the same thing is true in the three-camera television show where there is a live audience. There are four hours between the time that you get the actors up to performance and when you actually shoot it. You can't walk right onto the set and put your arms around an actor while the camera is rolling, whisper in his ear and make him cry, except in one-camera film.

•*JR:* What effect do you have upon pre-production?

•*JD:* In television, very, very little, although you are technically entitled to your first cut. In movies, you have tremendous amounts.

•*JR:* What are the major problems facing television as you see them, as a director?

•*JD:* See *Network.* I couldn't agree with it more. I think television is a horrendous monster and a totally immoral thing that is eating away our lives.

•*JR:* How do you see t.v. now, overall?

•*JD:* I see the whole thing as a tremendous political collusion between government and corporations, and their desires have nothing to do with either entertainment or education in a moral way. I think both of them, all of them are concerned with business, and government uses television to get publicity to get reelected.

Walter Doniger

If the term "dean of television directors" may be bestowed upon one person, then it is appropriate to Doniger. Over a period of four decades, he has worked in virtually all film genres from the American Air Force First Motion Picture Unit through over four hundred television series episodes. Doniger has written fifteen motion picture scripts and directed five features. His most recent work for television was Mad Bull *for CBS-TV.*

Currently, he is working with Robert Redford's Wildwood Productions on a feature film and is also writing for Roots—The Second Hundred Years, *being filmed in 1978.*

Television series: Marcus Welby; McCloud; The Man and the City; Night Gallery; Bracken's World; Maverick; Kung Fu; Ghost Story; The Bold Doctors; Griff; Owen Marshall; Sarge; The Virginian; Greatest Show on Earth; Mr. Novak; Travels of Jamie McPheeters; The Man Who Never Was; The Outlaws; Checkmate; Barnaby Jones; Lucas Tanner; Get Christie Love; Bat Masterson; Tombstone Territory; Highway Patrol, Jefferson Drum; Bold Venture; Cheyenne; *and many others, including 180 segments of* Peyton Place.

• *John Ravage:* Is there any difference in directing for television and directing for feature films?

• *Walter Doniger:* I think there is a difference. That difference between the top television directors and the top movie directors is not in talent, skill, or ability. It's in two different areas. One is that of self-discipline. The other is that of the speed with which decisions must be made.

The area of self-discipline is this. A motion picture director has only one fundamental necessity—that he make a successful film, one that makes money. If he does, no matter what his transgressions are in the eyes of the producer, the studio, the moneymen, or anybody else, there is total forgiveness. Probably he can go on to a bigger film, to higher pay, and bigger stars.

The situation is different for a television director. If he transgresses regularly the limitations of time and money—no matter how good the film is—he will not be directing again. The reasons here, as in features, are economic. Television has a very rigid financial structure. The network pays a certain amount of money for a license to show a segment of a series. That's all the studio gets from the film for that showing no matter how good it is—or isn't. It must make its profits—since usually the segment costs more than the network pays—hopefully in the future from reruns or various other worldwide releases of film.

This is the technique used by Universal. I did it twenty years ago with three television films which were combined and released as a single feature. But the organization making t.v. knows that initially no matter how good the film or what the cost it will receive only a preset amount back from the network.

Obviously the requirement to make a profit is the same for both television and motion pictures. But the mechanics of that requirement differ in each medium. Therefore, the demands on the director differ. If a director doesn't perform within certain time and money limits—no matter how good he is, no matter how high a quality product he delivers—he is, as I said, in trouble as a series television director.

In some extraordinary instances, the front office will say, "Hell, we'll take the risk on him in a big project." Thereby, if he is good enough, he may be able to jump out. But if you intend to work regularly in television, you must be a disciplined artist who will stay within the bounds of time and money, which are—in production terms—the same commodity.

Let's examine the other point—swiftness of creativity. As a director, one of the requirements in direction I make of myself is to know how I can do the day's work before I come to the stage. Hopefully, I will never use what I plan because something better will occur in the process on set. When I do something exactly as I planned it in the night before or during my preparation period—with the exception of highly technical action sequences—I feel a sense of failure. I like to come on a set and say, "Let's see what will happen." As I stated, I do this even though I have a plan.

Let me sidetrack to an anecdote which helped me learn its additional values. I directed Tony Quinn, a brilliant man, brilliant actor, enormously talented. If he had been born twenty-five years later he would have been one of the great stars. As a non-WASP at the time in our culture when being Clark Gable, Robert Montgomery, Robert Taylor, or equivalents were primary requirements for stardom—certainly not Mexican—he didn't achieve what he could have today. Most unfair—and anger making.

Tony Quinn would begin by asking you what you wanted him to do and promptly get in a fury over it. I found that the best thing to do was to be totally free to say, "I have no idea of what to do." Then we would undertake the exploration together. Thus he was a participant in the creation and didn't feel the kind of alien societal control which must have existed in his youth. The *process*, even though I may have had a plan and would use parts of it, was one of collaboration rather than direction and giving orders. I think we both enjoyed the process even though I worried about the clock. However, I found that we made better time this way than others on the show did.

But this led to another problem. For Tony to function—and he works on an energy which I think derives from anger—he would have to ignite himself before doing the scene. As a result of finding a method of working with him which I like to think was fruitful for both of us, sometimes other people got the brunt of his gearing himself up. He would find something to explode over and get his energies up. The performance always was worth it.

The point of this anecdote, I suppose, is that this method of being free in television only works if you don't violate the strictures of time and money. One good director on the Tony Quinn show did, and he has not worked at that studio since. This pressure tends to make directors—and others—play it safe. They shortchange freedom, looseness, and room in time and space for other people to interact and explore and not know—all invaluable to the creative process.

In terms of my other point—speed. In t.v. you cannot take the time to make decisions in the same way that you do in motion pictures. A director has to work at an intense rate. You have to find ways to do better work than someone else in the same time. You must use time efficiently and have several things happen simultaneously rather than do one thing at a time in a linear way. It is inefficient to wait for the actors to get made up, rehearse, then lay out the camera, then have the scene lit, etc. Instead I try to have several operations proceeding at once—*without chaos*.

So what I began to do was to look for certain cameramen who after a show or two would begin to understand the way I would like us to work while the scene was evolving with the actor and whoever else was around. Bringing something to the scene rather than rigidly laying it out in advance, I would give signals as to camera movement and positions. The cameraman and crew could then work simultaneously to conserve the time during which they would otherwise do nothing.

Sometimes, however, it would be necessary to rehearse without being able to do this in order to explore the scene. Of course it took time. On the other hand, I like to think that it lent a viability to the film, a reality and a sense of its happening, rather than mere predetermined staging. The actors would find their own freedom, where they felt comfortable. Then, within that comfort, I could impose very strict limits that allowed me to do scenes economically by various camera moves that saved setups—and in the end, time.

In terms of speed and quality, a real need for a t.v. director—any director today—is to understand really the meaning of the script. That sounds absurd, doesn't it? However, I became a director for that very reason after being a writer in feature films for years. I felt a general frustration that several big directors—names famous in film history—didn't know what the scripts I wrote were about.

One would think that since I'd been a writer in feature films for many years, it wasn't hard for me to know the meaning of the words. After all, words had been my profession for sixteen or eighteen years before I became a director. So I should be able to search out the hidden meanings, even the meanings that writers had set down without knowing fully what they were dealing with—because when a good writer is functioning well, he's often dealing with things, secret parts of himself, that he doesn't often recognize. And my job as a director is to find out what those secret parts of himself were. As a director I had to learn to do that. It isn't easy—at least for me. I was successful, I felt, when I was able to say to the writer, "I feel what you're writing about is this beyond the surface level. Do you agree?" In those good circumstances in television, where there was communication between the writer and the director, he would often say "No." Then he would think about it and say, "Well, yes, I think so," or "I haven't thought about that." Then he would in turn say, "Yes, I was dealing with that on an unconscious level."

But sometimes in spite of all the study, I or another director can come on set having really been wrong or not having understood certain things about a scene or character. The ground has disappeared beneath him—a terrifying feeling until you've had it happen often.

So, now, the television director who wants to achieve a certain degree of freedom has to find a way to free himself. That means freeing himself from fear of not knowing how he's going to do something. *This* means, in turn, being able to acknowledge to *other* people that he really doesn't know how to do something.

Even more, acknowledge it to himself, because the recognition of nonknowledge is in itself a freeing process.

The essence of the point I am making here is that a television director, ideally, has to come in with the subterfuge to himself of knowing nothing about how he's going to do a scene. Or if he truly doesn't know how to do it—or finds himself in error—be able to acknowledge that without fear.

Yet he must create an air that together they—all here and working together—will come to know how to do it. He must be able to make choices quickly, afford himself choices by being able to produce ideas quickly, be able to perceive what's happening with the actors in hopes that something that he could never have thought of will occur. It often does, let me tell you.

At the same time, hopefully, he is giving signals to the cameramen as to how the scene is going to be seen by the camera as the rehearsal is beginning to work, so the cameramen can start. At the same time, it is important to prevent chaos and to stay calm, because I don't think anyone works while being yelled at. There must be a confidence that whatever the problems, you and they will solve them, and though you may not know the answers totally, you'll find answers with everybody's help.

• *JR:* When you think of a television film and of a motion picture film, is there anything that you conceive of as different?

• *WD:* No, I try to think, "If this were a picture, how would I do it?" I make very few modifications. I will usually not do as many extreme long-shots on television as I might in films to get an effect. On the other hand, even on the television screen you can get impact from the long-shot. You just don't have the time for the extra rehearsals, for the exploration of the fourth of fifth idea instead of the second or third, for the twelfth or twentieth take instead of getting nervous at the seventh or eighth and stopping, or for the extra coverage that you might not even use. My approach to film is essentially a very simple one. What is it I really want to see in the most interesting way possible at this moment? How do I look at it in the most interesting way?

• *JR:* It's almost as if you're conceiving it from a cinematographer's viewpoint. Not, "What do I want to hear? What do I want the actors to do?" But how to stress this picture, regardless of whether it's television or film.

● *WD:* Absolutely not! I try to deal from content and meaning and feeling. I want to express them as fully as I can. So I deal with hearing and seeing and the selection of those elements. Essentially what you're doing is presenting an emotional communication between an image or a word and the receiver.

● *JR:* What's the best television work you think you've done? And why?

● *WD:* Hopefully the next thing I do.

● *JR:* I'm getting very diplomatic answers.

● *WD:* I'm not a diplomat. There are always individual pictures you like and are proud of. They change with time. It's hard for me to remember.

I want to think of tomorrow—not yesterday. You know, I've done almost two hundred *Peyton Place*s. I've probably done six or seven hundred films altogether; written fifteen or sixteen features; directed four or five. You also change your evaluation of "good."

I think I really began to understand my own philosophy of filmmaking when I was working on *Peyton Place*, though it has changed since. The reason for this is that I was working with the same people all the time. I had the authority to put together the kind of crew that I wanted. I was fortunate to work with the best cameramen, who were gamblers as I was. I was working with the same actors. Often communication was so good that words didn't have to be spoken. I would just say, "Well . . . " and the actor would respond, knowing what I meant. Ryan O'Neal was especially perceptive at that.

The people involved felt a great sense of pride in that show. It was probably the most successful show in the history of television. It got the greatest audiences at the time, and it was the only show that was ever rated number one by the polls three days in one week during the period it was on three days a week. There was a great *esprit de corps* among all the people.

There was also another very important thing that existed. On that program it was possible to gamble, be wrong, and make a mistake. There weren't the crises associated with being wrong that there are in a normal show. I had the freedom to make mistakes without the penalties that normally accrue.

That freedom derived out of a number of things. I directed the first show and set the style of visual approach and performance.

The style I developed for the show was a synthesis of all the things I'd learned over a number of years, but I went out over the edge. If I made a mistake, I could go back next week and correct it. All these things added together gave me the freedom to experiment. As a result, we made fewer mistakes, or at least I like to think I made fewer.

I don't mean my work was perfect by a long shot. I had freedom not to be certain and safe. For example, one of the things I remember—which was a great delight, even though we didn't use it in the film—was to do a shot that took place at a time when Mia Farrow's character was considering suicide. I just had a feeling that I wanted to do a shot of a blackbird high in a tree. Mia comes into the Peyton Place square. She holds up her hand to invite the bird to fly down. The bird flies down to her hand and comes to rest there. She looks at it, and then thrusts it away in fright.

When I conceived it, I couldn't tell you why I wanted to do that shot. I asked the executive producer, Paul Monash, who was superb to work with, if I could put the scene in. He gave permission to get the birds. I spent half a day of a two-and-a-half-day schedule getting that shot. Finally, I got it, after the bird gave us an enormous amount of trouble. After I finished it someone said, "Oh, I know why you wanted to do that shot. You were doing Mia seeking death and then rejecting it."

Somebody had to explain to me what I was doing . . . I didn't know. That freedom inside and out—hard to come by. This kind of freedom is the freedom you couldn't achieve, for example, today at Universal, where everybody in production would be too frightened. Twenty minutes after you started that shot the production office would be weeping and would be crawling all over your back.

• *JR:* Do you think the director should have, does have, or might have more control of content than the film director?

• *WD:* The television director certainly does have incredibly less control of content than the film director. Television is, after all, an advertising medium.

In motion pictures, the major criterion is "Will the film be a success? Will it make money?" There isn't the situation today that used to exist when I began in the business of "block-booking" before the antitrust decisions outlawed it. Then films could be guaranteed a modest—or immodest—profit by block-selling. Since that situation doesn't exist any more, every film is an enormous gamble. If a director seems to be able to guarantee a successful film, he has enormous control.

Television, in many ways, gives for nothing *almost* the same thing as does a motion picture. The necessity for a motion picture to be something distinct from that which they can get for free in t.v. means that the picture must be an extraordinary compilation of factors. This means that studios are always looking for the magic person who will rub those 128-140 pages with their paw and make it come out unique enough to force people into the theaters instead of sucking at the tube.

The man who accomplishes, as the French say, the *realization*, is the director. As a result he has gotten in films much more authority. There are feature directors who make a real contribution to the essential material of the film. There are directors who make marvelous contributions to the execution of the film. It all depends on the individual director. He may not literally write a word, but his understanding of life, truth, and feelings—and his interaction with the writer and the producer—affect the film enormously even when he doesn't change the words. Aside from the contribution to writing that a motion picture director makes, his contribution to the essence of the film is really what elevates one director above another.

All of this is a long, involved way of discussing the television director in terms of his control of the material. The television director is in a very, very difficult position. He or she has to say, "What price am I willing to pay?" Sometimes that price can be a severe one. You have to say, "Am I willing to take the position that I will do this kind of material, or I will *not* do this kind of material?"

It can begin with decision-making on the basic concept of a show itself. For example, there was a show years ago in which they made jokes about a German prison camp. . . . I could never do that program—even if I were asked, which I wasn't—because I could never feel that anything about the Nazis was very funny. I thought it diminished the whole terrible agony of what people went through during that period by making a joke of it.

So you make a basic decision about what you will do and won't do. If you make that decision, you pay a price for it. You don't work on that show. Afterwards, maybe one fellow tells somebody else, "Oh, he's difficult." Thereafter, you have problems in getting that show or others. That's one level of decision.

There's another level of decision which concerns the kind of people you want to work with. You have to decide if you will work with just any producer—or any actor—in order to get the money or the work. For example I choose not to work with Peter Falk because of his treatment of directors on *Columbo*. The same goes doubled in spades for Bobby Blake. Both are obviously talented men but . . .

● *JR:* You don't have any choice over crews, do you?

● *WD:* You have practically no choice over crews in t.v. I suppose I was one of the few people in dramatic television who not only had some choice, but really exercised that prerogative during my four years on *Peyton Place*. I built what I thought was the finest crew this business had ever seen. This crew, on days when I was feeling a little lazy, would come to me and say, "You're not doing the kind of work you should be doing. Why are you so lazy today?" I was grateful for that.

I had a script supervisor, which is the technical name for a script clerk, named Joan Erman. If she thought a take wasn't as good as it should be, she would come up to me and say, "Walter, I don't think you ought to print that. I think you ought to do another one." And she was usually right, too. I had a best boy to the key grip who'd come up to me and say, "Walter, you haven't really given us a tough shot yet, and we're getting bored." They liked difficult work and they would do it fast. We would do from twelve to fifteen pages in a day, shots with thirty moves, the crane, everything, and we'd be out by 4:30 or a quarter to 5, when everybody else was working 'til 7 or 8.

So I had a choice. In most cases directors have no choice whatsoever. They are strangers, visitors, or guests to the crews in most cases. In my case I was known as a tough director. I wasn't tough in the sense of being a yeller or a screamer. I just demanded performance from the crew. I expected everybody to do his job well and work a full day.

At the beginning of the season occasionally the director is consulted on crew. It happens more often on pilots. Then you have the choice of an individual script — doing it or not doing it—or waiting for the next assignment. And, that can be a very tough choice. First of all, that choice has to be exercised on the basis of the content of the script. Secondly, you must ask if the script is any good.

What does the word "good" mean? Whatever it means to me— whatever it means to you. Sometimes the same, sometimes different. I feel the director has a responsibility to himself and others on quality and content.

I was brought into *Marcus Welby* a couple of seasons ago to try to change the look of the show. People saw me as being principally concerned with imagery. I'm not, as I quite sharply answered you earlier. To me, imagery is a result of the communication you are trying to make. It begins with feeling. By no means do I mean to diminish imagery, because I think it is part of conveying a feeling.

At any rate, I was brought in on the show for that reason. They had a script which had to do with a certain kind of brain sur- gery—psychosurgery. It was something like a frontal loboto- my. From my own knowledge of prefrontal lobotomy in the past—people who had relatives to whom it was done and by my own personal perception and reading—I felt that any operation which cuts into the brain in order to make someone more docile to the society is doing something to the human being which shouldn't be done.

This film script fundamentally took the position that this was a good procedure for the patient. I felt this film shouldn't be made and I said it shouldn't. The producers said that doctors who did it said it was good procedure. It wasn't like prefrontal lobotomy, anyway. I talked to several doctors who weren't the ones who did it. They told me in a sense it was "son of prefrontal lobotomy." Prefrontals are generally not done today. I went back and said, "Look, I cannot do this film because it takes an approving position on a questionable medical procedure. I will not do this film and I don't think you people should do it." They said, "Well, we're gonna do it."

So these are the basic decisions you have to make about the individual script. And I made it.

Now, the other kind of decisions . . . As you say, is it worth spending my time to get some money to make a film at the end of which I will say, "Why did I do this? Why did I use my time, my energy, my life juices for no reason?" This doesn't mean that you're making masterpieces all the time; you're not. But you have to decide your own threshold.

• *JR:* Have you ever refused an assignment?

• *WD:* I just told you I did. Scores of times. Here is another occasion which worked out differently. I was to direct a segment of *Owen Marshall*. It happened to be about a boy who had been a draft dodger and gone to Canada. It also happened to be a murder story, but the start of it was about a draft dodger coming back and saying how wrong he was to oppose the Vietnam War. This was long before an antiwar position was popular. I read the script and I thought, "Well, gee, I can't face myself or any of my young friends if I did a script like this." Yet I feel everybody—just as I do—has the right to make up his own mind about what he or she wants to do.

I went back to the producer. I said, "Look, I can't do this script. Get another director." He asked me why. I said, "You know there's no point in getting into it with you people because it's a fundamental difference in viewpoint."

"We have a commitment with you," he said. "We have a right to an explanation."

I said, "Well, I can't do it, because it violates what I believe."

He asked me why—the producer was a very nice man but not a man of very decided viewpoints—and I told him.

He said, "Well, we can't put a show on that says somebody who is a draft dodger and goes to Canada is a hero."

I said, "Well, you have the right to decide what shows you'll put on. I'll decide what shows I'll shoot."

Then he said, "Well, I've got to call the executive producer."

The executive producer came down. I explained to him why I couldn't do the show. He said, "Well, we have a problem. You know, with the network and everything else."

I said, "I think you'll have a problem with other people besides me, because if I feel this way, there must be somebody else who does too. I can't be the only person who feels this way."

He said, "Is there a solution?"

In this case I thought the easiest thing would be to refuse to do it. But since he was open to finding a reasonable solution that I could live with, I was obliged to try. We found a solution which was acceptable to me and him. We managed to persuade the network to go along with it too. I was able to do a film that I could live with, that took a compassionate position toward a draft dodger.

The film was one of the first that said a man who was a draft dodger and went to Canada perhaps had more strength—in his own way—than someone who made a different choice and let himself be drafted. These are the decisions you make in television—or don't make. You're never going to make any really enormous breakthroughs, but you struggle and you make some compromises, and you do your best. I like to think it helps change things.

I've been lucky in that people who hire me know they will deal with the question of rewriting. I don't mean I personally rewrite in most cases. I may ask for changes that I can justify in terms of making a better film. I won't do the assignment if I feel the script isn't good. I've not gotten certain assignments because of this— and no longer work for the *Owen Marshall* producer—but I'd do it all over again.

It's not a new conflict in any society. I like living well. I like earning money. But I like to think there are other things that are important. When I look at the final cut of a film, I don't want to throw up. It's not often that you do something that sings for you. But it's nice to keep trying.

● *JR:* When you look at the present state of television offerings, what do you think?

● *WD:* The answer to what I think is really explained and clarified by where I am at this moment. One makes a decision and he hopes that he will keep it. I decided that I was just not going to do any more series hour television, though I don't feel the same way about the long-form.

You see me here at a feature production company because I made that decision to not do any more hour television. To implement it, I sat down and wrote a feature script. Robert Redford and Walter Coblenz, head of his company, read it and asked me to write a script for them from a book they bought. I have just finished the first draft and it's really like being transplanted to Nirvana. My research travels on it took me to Washington, London, and Belfast.

The circumstances of it happening were nice. On the very last day of shooting *Delvecchio*—where I worked with a superb actor, Judd Hirsch—I had told the various people at the studio that under no circumstances was I going to do any more television work. Walter Coblenz on that last day called and asked me if I would come to work. So, it was like being rescued from the railroad tracks. Otherwise, I would just simply have gone home, sat down at the typewriter, and hopefully written another script.

These decisions are very personal ones. As an older man, I was no longer willing to use up whatever time I have left doing hour television.

• *JR:* What drove you to this?

• *WD:* What I saw were essentially decent, talented people being put under enormous pressure to produce—at unreasonable production budgets and within severe time limitations—a film product. Most of them want to do good work and suffer severely under the pressure. They just don't have the time to do the things that they recognize should be done. These producers, directors, writers are not stupid people. They're not untalented people. They are a part of a whole chute of producers, directors, writers, a whole c-h-u-t-e . . .

• *JR:* Interesting word you chose.

• *WD:* . . . of scripts, waiting to be made, that must meet an air date. This puts the producers of television in the worst position of all. They endure pressure from everybody—the front office, the production department, directors who want changes, the networks, the series stars—to do so many different things. There just isn't the time or money. A lot of them, to get through this agony, have to work sixteen or seventeen hours a day.

We are dealing with the essential nature of television. It isn't that the people who make it are untalented or insensitive. You're dealing with people who are in the position of Charlie Chaplin in *Modern Times,* when he was at the assembly belt. He just could not slow down because the thing got away from him. So does t.v. . . .

It forces us to work at a certain speed and do certain things which make unreasonable demands upon other human beings. I found myself doing the same thing with the crew. I do it *not* by yelling or screaming. I never sit down the whole work day, people have told me. I suppose it's true. I never stop for an instant and try to keep the crew going that way. But that's the only way to pack more into the number of hours that you have available.

So in t.v. all of us—fairly decent people—commit one kind of inhumanity or another upon each other. It's part of the machine of television. I guess that is one of the other reasons I would rather not continue. I get up, work, go home, have dinner, prepare for the next day, sleep, get up and go to work, drive myself, go home, have dinner, etc., etc. If I'm going to do this, it has to be something that I feel is going to be really and truly worthwhile, once in a while. By my measurement, whatever that measurement is, it wasn't worthwhile enough. I decided to stop.

● *JR:* One of the considerations of any theatrical format is that of the audience. The director of theater knows he's going to be watched by a sophisticated audience; producers of feature films know their audience. In television, obviously, none of those things apply. Television directors are making a product for an illiterate, tasteless audience that drives them to make compromises. Do you have any comment to make on that kind of observation?

● *WD:* I don't accept the validity of that observation. You're always making compromises in life and film. I really believe in Rousseau's social contract. As soon as two people come together, they compromise. You drive down the right-hand side of the street instead of whichever side you would like, which is a compromise. You drive at a certain speed, according to signs. There are always limitations of some sort or another.

The real question is which limitations are valid—those for you and for me are not always the same. Thus, a dilemma. I disagree with your question because it is not the illiterate, tasteless audience that drives directors to compromises. It is the advertising and structure of t.v.—an advertising medium.

I think that the audience is not that dissimilar, whether educated or uneducated. You're dealing with what's happening in society or the world. So are they—consciously or unconsciously. What are the feelings people have? How does a piece of dramatic material reflect those feelings? I think art has a symbiotic relationship to life in that they feed upon each other.

I was talking earlier about the television scripts that are good. They are scripts in which I perceived that the writer consciously or unconsciously made some contact with himself, so that he is reflecting his own life. Thereby, in the tradition of "Let one ant tell the story of the whole colony or one soldier, the whole war," the writer is reflecting something in the society and the world. In the same sense, I think that the actor who is a star in a certain time reflects what is happening in the culture. That is the appeal of the star. The public recognizes, unconsciously, that the star is they— and they are the star.

● *JR:* Are there problems facing the television director that must be resolved before you would be interested in going back to it?

● *WD:* Let me begin with a picture called *Lawrence of Arabia*. That was a picture made for the big screen by one of the great screen directors, David Lean. I was very curious as to what would happen when that picture was shown on the little screen. I looked at it. I must say I was as enthralled, and almost as satisfied— surprisingly enough to me—as if it were on a big screen. Maybe there was a small difference. But not the kind that I had anticipated. The film worked. It is in a sense an affirmation of my feeling in an absolute sense that the differences between the two images, t.v. and feature, are not ones of craft, skill, technique, content, or anything like that. Certainly it would be marvelous, however, if there were a big screen for television, with more than the present number of resolution lines. But to me, that's not the determinant of the problem for the director, the writer, the producer, or even the studio involved in t.v.

The problem, as I see it, is this: Television is, essentially, not a product in itself. Television is a medium which has as its function selling goods. In the long run, no matter what exceptions there are, television's function is to sell an automobile, to sell toilet paper, to sell cosmetics, to sell tampons—to sell *another* product. So it is a service medium.

Now, when you are a service medium, you may be producing a product—but its function is to serve the product to which it is a service. Television film on the networks is a service through which advertisers sell their product.

No matter how wonderful that t.v. film is, if it offends one half of 1 percent of the audience, the man who is paying for that program says, "They are going to connect my product with that show. That means I've lost one half of 1 percent of my buyers."

If it happens twenty times, that means he lost 10 percent of his business. It's a reasonable conclusion they'll buy another similar product. It's eminently reasonable for an advertiser to insist that no product be put on television which causes his product to be offensive in the eyes of those who may buy it. That's the only reason he's buying television time—to sell his product. Thus the t.v. dilemma on meaningful content. . . .

There are certain exceptions to this rule. You'll find the large companies, when they are making enormous profits—like Xerox, IBM, General Motors—have special programs which sometimes are controversial. You will also notice it is when their profits have been incredible for many years that they make these films. They have cut down on these films recently since their profits have not been so monumental. Or the oil companies may try to ameliorate their image with "good work."

You'll find that this is the pattern throughout network commercial television. There are some exceptions. After all, television comes to us on our sets by virtue of a bestowal to the networks and stations of the right to broadcast.

This right is granted by us, the people of the United States, through a delegate, the United States government, to the networks. There has to be some kind of evidence that they are performing a socially beneficial function and occasionally there is pressure on them to evince that. There are all kinds of regulations in the FCC concerning that necessity—many of which are not conformed to.

● *JR:* The place of the PBS: I've had only one director out of the dozen I've talked to so far who was pleased with PBS. One loves working on it. He said that he went to PBS to "wash Warner Bros. out of his head." This man may be the biggest moneymaker in the business, but most of the people I've talked to say that they don't want to be involved with PBS. Have you ever had any contacts with PBS?

• *WD:* I have some contact with PBS. As a matter of fact, they were talking to me about the possibility of doing a five-hour show on some material that I have. I think, however, there are many problems in PBS. In some ways the problems are different, because PBS is governmental. Wherever government enters, I think, there are problems—just as there are problems wherever industry enters. PBS experiences a different kind of censorship. Maybe not as overt as that of commercial television, but more subtle. In some areas it is even overt. All you have to do is listen to a program director at PBS discuss the problems of member stations' program attitudes to realize it.

There are other problems, such as the limited money available for PBS. To some extent this is being mitigated by the entry of organizations like Arco, Atlantic Richfield, Xerox, and IBM, who will give partial or total money for these projects. Earlier I explained what I feel are some of their reasons for giving money. How does this affect programming? There's an old saw that's very applicable. "He calls the tune who pays the fiddler."

In societies such as ours, the man who pays the money for something will have an enormous say in determining what goes on and doesn't go on. In Russian society a different kind of censorship goes on. As a generality I hate censorship in every form because it has an insidious purpose which it conceals behind attacks on porno films, *Hustler,* nudity, and whatever is on the outer edges.

The purpose of that censorship? I think every society is dedicated to preserving itself in one way or another. Certainly we saw that in the 60s when society crushed the youth revolution with a willingness to kill, if necessary. It is exemplified by our loathsome former President Nixon who was responsible for many of those deaths by his implicit and expressed approval of varied shootings of students. Also his t.v. statement that if he says it, it is the law.

I think in the end, any society is so involved with its own preservation, it will certainly have a tendency to not put on artistic materials which appear critical or inimical to its own apparent interest. Any society that's structured to preserve itself will absorb and adopt the elements that tend to oppose it, so as to diffuse the opposition. If not, it will attempt to destroy those critical elements. Since the function of the artist is to examine *critically*, therein lies the dilemma for both.

• *JR:* Where does Walter Doniger learn his skills?

• *WD:* Basically, living and feeling my life. Technically, I spend time looking more at theatrical films than I do at television. I feel that the people who are involved in theatrical films have more time and more room, for all the reasons I've previously stated, to try and do better things, besides being chosen for their talent. I think I can learn more from them than I can from other places.

I know it sounds immodest, but I want to go to sources I can learn from, rather than places where, in a sense, they imitate things that I do. On the last show, *Delvecchio*, the other directors were told to imitate me. I don't like it, even though I'm flattered by it. I'd never work a show where I was told to imitate someone else.

• *JR:* How about writers? Any particular television writers that stick in your mind?

• *WD:* I think the saddest situation in t.v. is for writers who do hour segments. I don't want to talk individually about them. I'm not talking about writers who work in long-form television. There is room for real creativity there.

However, I think that hour television is one of the most destructive things that's ever happened to the writer. It's structured so that if you stay in hour television, it seems that you cannot really survive without an enormous amount of pain, an enormous amount of conflict, and some personal character destruction.

If you look at such a simple thing as how assignments are given out you'll get some idea. It's really like the land rush in the days of the old West. On a certain date when the new season starts, all the writers line up. The gun goes off. They all rush to the various offices of the various producers and try to sell ideas and get assignments for the first half of the season. What they are involved in doing is selling, not writing. Writing is a process in depth, I think, not surface. It is feeling and thinking—not huckstering. It is vertical rather than horizontal. It's a long, hard process—unless it's an idea which has been germinating within you for a long time.

Unfortunately, because of the seasonal, starting gate nature of television, writers have to sell a lot of ideas at once. Their ideas have to be attention-getters—loud farts—not subtle ideas and feelings of depth. The writer has to *sell* something and that means he must be verbally quick and facile in order to get the assignment. *They're involved in selling rather than writing.* They're involved in pleasing an enormous number of people in a few sentences. They're involved in all kinds of strictures of hour television, of what the series lead can and can't do, format problems, etc. They're involved in the big dilemma of telling stories in which the central character doesn't change. This means you're driven to cop, lawyer, doctor, private-eye series because at least he has an action.

The essence of most good drama is some kind of change in the central character. You see this in most good pictures. You see some kind of growth. Yet, in television, by necessity, the running character is set and unchanging. He is the same all the time.

Some writers try to find change in other characters. But to turn out ten to twelve scripts a year and have three or four scripts going at the same time is a terrible load. To have three or four producers calling forces some writers to refuse to answer the phone because they can't get the work out in time. Because of subsequent commitments, they try to avoid doing as much rewriting as possible. They have to move on to the next thing or get it done by a certain date in order to make a certain self-determined amount of money. All these things are terrible, terrible burdens on the psyche and character of the writer.

Each time a director or producer comes in and opens his mouth about a script, the writer's heart drops. I've seen it happen. The writer's silently saying to himself, "They're gonna make me do more work and that will delay my doing the next thing."

Of course, story editors do a lot of the rewriting. But the pressure mounts on them, too. How they manage as well as they do, I don't know.

● *JR:* Make the same evaluation of producers as you have done of writers.

● *WD:* Producers are the key element in any television story or series. The producer makes the final decisions in the actual area of making films—aside from executive and network input. That is as it should be, I feel. I believe in the chain of authority. I think someone has to make those final decisions. He is the continuing element. He really determines the form and shape of the series.

Sometimes there are two producers—the "production produc-er" and the "script producer." These men are the prime determi-nants of what a series will be like. They have to be able to rewrite unless there is a *writing* story editor. That's why one of them—if there are two—will be a former writer and do a lot of writing.

These men have a tremendous problem. They have to cope with the network. They have to cope with the front office. They have to cope with the production department, which is interested in protecting itself for its own survival in terms of costs. The producer constantly has to struggle with the production depart-ment over costs.

There are very few unit managers who approach a project saying, "How can we make this good?" There are some, and they are a pleasure to work with. Jack Terry at Universal Studios is one of them—and that is a tough place to be one. He always helps find the way to reconcile the conflict. Jerry Zeisimer is another. But most are interested in protecting themselves from being accused of spending too much money. At the very least they want to protect themselves by going on record as saying, "If you do this, it's going to be a disaster in cost." But as I said, there are some who are wonderful, who find creative solutions, and they are exhilarating to work with.

The producer has to deal with the star. The star of a series is the one essential man. Everybody else can be disposed of . . . even the producer. In any confrontation, the star, if he wants to, must win. So the producer also has this problem. He has to live with the star next week, and the week after that, and the week after that. Yet he must control a situation in which he does not have ultimate control. I think it's the most difficult job in television, and I don't see how most of them stand it.

Now that I thumb back over the words I have been speaking, I have a question to ask. What the hell am I doing in a business like this? Just lucky, I guess. . . .

Lamont Johnson

First entering the business as an actor in a variety of television, film, and stage roles, Johnson has directed plays for the legitimate stage (The Egg, Yes Is for a Very Young Man) *as well as opera, television, and feature films such as* Lipstick, The McKenzie Break, The Last American Hero *and his most recent film,* One on One. *His long-form television assignments include* That Certain Summer, My Sweet Charlie, The Execution of Private Slovik, *and* Fear on Trial.

Television series: Peter Gunn; Have Gun, Will Travel; The Defenders; The Twilight Zone; *and* Profiles in Courage.

• *John Ravage:* When you direct for television, what goes through your mind; what do you do?

• *Lamont Johnson:* I've done five television shows in eight years now, and they've all been specials: *My Sweet Charlie, That Certain Summer, Private Slovik, Birdbath,* and *Fear on Trial.* Five specials. They've been either two and a half or three hours long. You do have considerably more latitude than in the shorter forms. You have a good deal more leeway in terms of budget and time. Even so, it's a vastly collapsed shooting schedule. *Slovik* cost $1.3 million, which made it a very low-priced movie these days, but two and a half years ago that was a sizeable budget, and the film required a three-hour form in order to justify the costs. Still, we did it in twenty-four days, and that's just incredible when you stop and think of all the moves—eighty-one sets in twenty-four days.

I showed it at the Directors' Guild and I asked some of my old heroes to come, see it, and comment. Fritz Lang had been interested in the case to begin with, and he came. The next day he called me and talked for two hours. I was very impressed with him. He asked me all kinds of questions, made critiques, did all kinds of interesting didoes with it. Then he said, "Tell me, how long was the schedule?" I said twenty-four days. "Now, I will never believe anything you tell me again," he said. It was incomprehensible to him. We shot the film in Camp Roberts; San Luis Obispo, California; the Queen Mary, in Long Beach; in Pasadena; Burbank; and a week in Canada. You don't have any idle time, any spare time. The secret to doing exciting television, I mean quality television, is to have an extraordinarily well-organized and well-rehearsed production.

I never rehearse less than ten days, which is very rare for the bulk of television. For specials we rehearse ten days; then you're ready for all eventualities. You're faced with the tricks of weather, or lights, or the exigencies of being on location. Additionally, you're not hung up with trying to get actors to realize a moment that is essential to the script. You've worked out the foundation, the skeletal relationships, and all the moments quite thoroughly ahead of time, so that you're well prepared. You have a sense of the whole. When you get to the location, you get additional input, additional excitement, energy, and vitality out of the location. Instead of being hung up by it, worried about it, you're ready to adapt to it. So other than the fact that you really have to plan well, I don't think about much of anything else. You don't spend a lot of time on very big productions, although there was a great deal of that in *The Execution of Private Slovik.* Of course it wasn't miles of terrain and it wasn't huge mob scenes.

•*JR:* You don't think differently about the number of set-ups or the use of two-shots?

•*LJ:* No. Quite frequently I'll go with the master that will go three, four, or five minutes; just one piece, *Fear on Trial,* had a lot of those. Very much a motion picture. In the films, sometimes that happens; sometimes the filmmaker or writer is the director. In the television I have witnessed as I've been around over the past couple years, watching directors direct, directors rewrite dialogue.

•*JR:* What do you think the director's responsibility is to the content of the television material that he is filming or taping?

•*LJ:* To make it as credible and as rich as time will permit. To take the material—before you're in rehearsal even—to scrutinize it closely for credibility and for values and get as much out of it as possible. To work in combination with a good writer, a good collaborator, or, if necessary, yourself. Do it yourself if you have to. I've done both.

•*JR:* Of course you had the playwriting background to do it, and many directors don't.

•*LJ:* And as an actor I use improvisation to a great degree. Levinson and Link were a little nervous about that because it seemed to imply a dissatisfaction with their words. I finally convinced them that was not the case, that we could work as collaborators or cowriters on it. The director is writing with light and people on the film just as much as the authors are writing on the typewriter, visualizing the same. They finally came into a couple of improvisational rehearsals we were having, and they loved it.

We got some notions for missing links in the script; things that had bothered me were filled out. We, together with the actors, discussed our fantasies based on some of the clues we got of the diaries and letters of Slovik and his wife. We filled in a few spots and then improvised a fight, which is a quarrel in the night, when he was sneaking out of the house. It was not in the script originally. We improvised that.

There needs to be this kind of abrasion. The frustrations and the tortures of the characters' problems have to be there, or an audience is not really going to care.

So we improvised and then had Levinson and Link come in and watch; they were terribly turned on. They said, "Let's go home and work on it." They did. We took that script, that scene, and we improvised on it until we shot it. That's one of the best relationship scenes in the picture. It reveals the heart of their marriage and their relationship.

A script is never finished, as far as I'm concerned. We're working on one right now; I just looped in a line from one character so that it clarifies the scene. So it goes. I work on the script right up to final edit.

•*JR:* Why do you work in a form that many others have rejected as inadequate for their own expression?

•*LJ:* Possibly because of the material. If the material is good, then I'd rather do it no matter. I've done a little something in every medium and quite a great deal in most, and I would never turn down an extraordinarily challenging television assignment. I get all kinds of scripts and my agent is under strict instructions not to turn away anything just because it's a television special. At this stage of the game, I'm sure I wouldn't do a segment of anything— and I haven't since 1970. However, I certainly read specials, and I read books that are considered for specials, projects that people are interested in developing because they are good pieces of material. I would like to have a crack at some of the more remarkable material, but there is very little of it around.

•*JR:* Who is your audience?

• *LJ:* I'm very pleased with the fact that provocative material (as provocative as we're allowed on television) gets to an enormous audience. I am elated at the ratings, and sixty or seventy-five million people spent the entire three hours with *Slovik*. It's not an easy show; it's an ordeal kind of show. They weren't a bunch of cretins, or bubblegum poppers sitting there watching *Slovik*; they were relatively serious. I think that we heavily underestimate the numbers of people who are interested in stimulating television fare; they're not dumbos just sitting, staring vacantly at the screen, cracking their fourth bottle of Coors.

I just think that there's a terrific audience out there, and the response I got from these programs has been most rewarding. For instance, when Judith Crist saw *Slovik,* she had been alarmed by what had happened when *My Sweet Charlie* came out and it got enormous ratings, great notices. Then Universal, three weeks after it was on the air, put it into a trial run in theaters in New York—two theaters at some remote end of Manhattan Island with an ad campaign that said "See the Biggest Event of the Decade on Television." Now who is going to pay three bucks to see a television event that they may have already seen and, furthermore, one they know will be repeated? Terrible campaign. So, it didn't do any business. Crist had thought that was stupid and had written an article about it. She called me when she saw *Slovik*. She gave it a great review and said that she was pleased that the film was not to be run in the theaters. Sixty to seventy million people will see this extraordinary show on television, and if you got ten thousand people into motion picture theaters around the country, you'd be lucky. Nobody's going to pay the money to see that difficult a show. She's right.

There seems to be some correlation between the things that get me excited and make me want to do television and what turns on an audience, because the same thing happened with *That Certain Summer.* A quieter piece of chamber music you never saw; it's very uneventful, unsensational, a character piece. It's a quartet, four people; that's about it. No big production numbers, nothing. We had an enormous rating and incredible quantities of print. The *New York Times* did three totally different approaches to covering it. One, the Sunday before it was on, and others on two

Sundays after, with follow-up articles and letters. It was not that the subject of homosexuality hadn't been dealt with before, because it had. In a veiled fashion I had dealt with it in a *Judd for the Defense* in about 1968: a father was terrified that his son was having a homosexual relationship with his buddy—they were very fond of each other—but the father had seriously unresolved homosexual problems himself and was projecting this relationship onto his son. It's a very powerful story. That was on five years before, so I couldn't quite swallow "Oh what a revolutionary breakthrough." I must say we only said the word "homosexual" once and in a very roundabout reference. It was the first case of its being openly discussed as a real social problem. That probably got to the large audience.

• *JR:* Judging from the titles of the shows you have directed, *The Defenders, Judd, Slovik,* one can identify a common thread of important social concerns of the day. For instance, *Slovik* came at a time in which we were all questioning ourselves about the Vietnamese War. Is that a fair evaluation?

• *LJ:* Well, certainly that's attracted me in television, and I do get involved in events of the world we live in. They are intriguing to me and I can be enthusiastic about them. I have to get enthusiastic in order to do the very hard work involved. I love it and I can only love it if I really have a strong feeling about it. I have to care a good deal. I've been lucky because for quite a few years now I've been able to say, "No, I don't want to do that, I want to do this." It's nice. So I've chosen to do television projects that really excite me in place of some movie things that I've been offered that haven't really excited me at all. I think I've generally had better luck with the television specials than with the films I've chosen.

• *JR:* Were the exceptions dealing with the same kinds of considerations?

• *LJ:* Not really, no. I think *Last American Hero* is the best movie I've made so far, although I'm very fond of what I'm doing right now [*One on One*]. They have a sort of similarity; they deal with the ethics and the morality of our culture as they relate to athletics. This film deals with a kid who comes to full acknowledgment of values that he has conveniently tucked away because he has been raised on a compulsive ethic of success or death. When he gets to college, a lot of other things rush at him. His mind opens up; his emotions open up; he finds that life is very rich indeed and that being a jock isn't the alpha and omega of existence.

• *JR:* Right now, the major dramatic form on television is situation comedy, yet the types of programs you have done have been successful. Could you comment upon this?

• *LJ:* Well, I find relief in doing a good comedy too. I love comedy. I've done a lot of it in the early days of my television directing, but I think comedy can be every bit as stimulating, every bit as illuminating, and perhaps—in the classic instances—every bit as important to the world as tragedy or straight dramas. Comedy is deeply rooted in character conflict; both parties in a comic situation care desperately about a given end and are working toward it with great seriousness. The result is an absurdity, and that's what I find in the best kind of comedy. That's what makes really interesting comedy for me, rather than "gag" comedy. Occasionally a gag is fun. If a gag seems organic to a scene, instead of just tacked on, gags are great. But a series of gags intended for a built-in laugh—I'm not fond of that kind of comedy. It's not my style; it's not my thing. In 1960 and '67 I did comedy live. It was sold and I loved it. I was signed to be a producer-director, *the* producer-director. The company was interested in having me continue the quality. I said that I would not sign a long-term contract; I wanted to be able to do plays, operas, movies, whatever. They tried to change it into something else, a *Lucille Ball Show,* and the character we had simply could not adapt. After three episodes, I quit cold. I just simply did not want to put up the struggle of manufacturing a gag show. It died in about thirteen weeks.

• *JR:* Is your attitude toward or your treatment of actors different from theater or film directors?

• *LJ:* I think all good directors must have a strong relationship with their actors. There are wonderful directors who have been cutters; cameramen who have had what it takes to create a climate of functioning creativity for actors. What is necessary is the establishment of mutual trust and daring, of allowing yourself to really go all the way on a line interpretation. Not just to be safe, but to behave as one does in a theater when you have a period of six to eight weeks of rehearsal, where you can try anything, fall on your ass, try it again . . . sleep on it, fail miserably, and come back to find something exciting. That's the only way you get interesting work. It's like learning anything in life, you have to do it clumsily, hurt yourself, grieve, rage, and break through to your fresher, more creative self. Elsewise, you're simply turning out the convenient and the easy, the sure thing. It's getting involved all the way that makes it work.

• *JR:* Since you work in the long-form specials that aren't restricted by the traditional pre-production, shooting, post-production time limits, what is your directing process?

• *LJ:* I like to try everything. In the early days, I had just come out of *Matinee Theater,* where I had started directing live television; there was no tape, no turning back. I did seventy-eight of those in two years. Then I went directly from that into outdoor things like *Have Gun, Will Travel* and some westerns, about fifteen of those in two or three years. I had a good time in those years. *Peter Gunn* was a gas. I loved working with Blake Edwards. It was great fun because, generally, the scripts were perfectly terrible. You had wonderful people to work with and you improvised. I'd go to complain to Blake Edwards; I'd say, "Oh, great, cut it. Do something else. Surprise me." I had a great sense of challenge, and I did something quite bizarre, which became the hallmark of that show. It was a really bizarre kind of show.

• *JR:* How do you direct actors?

• *LJ:* I approach them before entering rehearsal. By the time I start rehearsing I have done already a fair amount of reading and discussion, and I've developed a relationship of sharing with them so that they're ready to pour out their innermost thoughts and feelings. I respond in kind and note that we have a sense of mutuality about the script. The rehearsals are always very lively— a lot of stimuli back and forth; they're fun. They're the most fun things about movies. Actual shooting is drudgery: getting it right technically, tricks of shooting on location. So you really have to be in touch with what you're doing with the actors. You have to have a very close bond with them. I can't recall, I literally *can't* recall, having antipathy for any of the actors I have worked with in recent years.

• *JR:* You are being really very nice, or you're one of the rarest directors . . .

• *LJ:* No, no. I find that one can develop a mutual

enthusiasm for a project that transcends dislikes. I don't mean to say that I just love everybody I've worked with. There are some I wouldn't walk across the street to meet or wouldn't lift a phone to speak to again throughout the rest of my life. But for a particular need, a particular purpose, and particular show, yes, they were wonderful. Therefore, an enthusiasm for the event created a relationship between the two of us that transcended any distaste we might have for each other. There've been only two actors that come to mind in my whole directing time who were so abrasive that I either left or got rid of them.

Seymour "Buzz" Kulik

Kulik, like most television directors of his generation, began in New York City by directing live programs in the 1950s, such as Playhouse 90, Lux Video Theater, *and* Kraft Theater. *He saw the importance of simultaneous production and direction; therefore, he has usually worked in both capacities.*

Kulik's most recent work has been the direction of long-form programs like The Lindbergh Kidnapping, Vanished, *and* Kill Me If You Can.

Television series: The Twilight Zone; Doctor Kildare; The Defenders; Climax; *and* Dick Powell Playhouse.

●*John Ravage:* What differentiates television directing from films?

●*Buzz Kulik:* To a great extent I think it's basically the same thing. Whether one directs for the stage, or for the big screen, or for television, all of which I've done, or two people in an elevator, or in traffic or wherever—to a great extent it's basically the same. There are different techniques that have to be employed in each medium. As an example, some years ago I appeared before the California State Dramatic Teachers Association with Daniel Mann. Danny was asked about the close-up, and he said, "Well, I'm very concerned about the number of close-ups that I use in telling my story, because when I do go to a close-up I want to make a point. I want to punctuate. I want to bring the audience's attention to the moment. I use it for that purpose. I'm very, very careful to not overdo it, because I don't want to lose the effect. In my films you'll see precious few close-ups, just enough to punctuate." The question was then asked of me, as a television director, and I said, "Well, I've got to use the close-up just to get the audience to see what's going on. Because it's not an enormous screen, it's a nineteen-inch set in the home."

● *JR:* So you are constantly aware of the frame and its limitations?

● *BK:* Yes, and I can find other ways of punctuating, you see. One does use the close-up on the big screen. In features you have to be very careful that you don't overdo their use because you'll lose the point of view. In our medium we have to do that all the time in order to get the public merely to see what is happening, and so we have to find different ways of making those punctuations. I think the differences are ones of technique. The basic business of directing is fairly much the same in either format.

● *JR:* Do you have any techniques which you consciously try to use?

● *BK:* No. Each play requires a different point of view, from the standpoint of the style of the acting, the style of the lighting, the style of the editing, each one. *Brian's Song* required one sort of thing. *The Lindbergh Kidnapping* required another. I'm preparing a television film now called *Kill Me If You Can*, the story of Caryl Chessman. We're going to start shooting in January, and I've been worrying for the last month now, working out a style. Normally that kind of show requires a kind of a dark mood, because it's a disturbing piece. However, so much of this takes place in a prison cell that you can't be too dark, because it will become boring. What you are trying to say with the film will determine the particular style.

● *JR:* You don't go to it with any bag of tricks that say "These are Buzz Kulik's Trademarks"?

● *BK:* No, no, I don't. I learned that in live television when I used to do a show called *Climax*. I did one every other week. Fifty-two productions live. I discovered very quickly that if out of the twenty-six I was required to do I could do three that were really very good, that was an enormously big percentage. The great number of them were fairly rotten, and I discovered early that I could hide the fact that the story was lousy by doing all kinds of tricky things with the camera. I thought that if I kept moving fast and shuffling my feet, they wouldn't see me, but it didn't work. A good story is a good story, and a lousy story is a lousy story. As a matter of fact, in most cases trickery only pointed up the deficiency. There are certain ways that I like to stage scenes, but that's as far as it goes. I've been fortunate in having such a varied assortment of things to do that I let the story determine the form.

• *JR:* When you've got good material, you've got the breaks, true?

• *BK:* There's no getting around that. In my opinion, the best cast and the best direction and the best cameramen and the best of the best of the best can maybe make a lousy story 5 percent better, but they're never going to take something that was really rotten and make it great; don't let anybody tell you that. That's what it comes down to.

• *JR:* And this brings the writer into the process. If the director is generally overlooked, forgotten, missed or whatever, the writer is more so?

• *BK:* In live television that wasn't the case. In live television the writer was a very, very important contributor. What we did in *Climax* and *Playhouse 90* was to bring the writer out here and give him a per diem. He stayed all the way through the production; he was on hand to have his input, have his say to protect his material. If changes were to be made, he changed them. In the motion picture business, you can't just do that anymore. You have to pay them another fee, and it becomes costly. I don't think it's *that* costly but the motion picture industry doesn't believe me. However, there are also some writers who, at their own cost, will stay with you. I'm going to work with John Gay now, who is one of the best men in our business, and John stays. John volunteers his time, which is money. He's going to spend six to eight weeks for free, but he feels that the end result is worth it.

• *JR:* I've had directors tell me that writers aren't that interested anyway. They've got to sell twelve scripts; they can't take the time. Yet some writers have told me just exactly the opposite.

• *BK:* In order to make a decent living he has to keep writing. There are a number of guys who really are not interested in doing that. We have the same thing in the Directors' Guild. You would be surprised at the number of television directors who don't want to cut their own pictures because they would prefer to be off shooting something else. In our last two negotiations we've been able to get great concessions from the producer; the right of first cut. Not only that, but the right to show the finished product to the producer and explain a cut to him. Still, we have a number of men who just don't want to take advantage of it. Because it's a big, big problem for us, we've been talking of assessing penalties on those members who will not do that. We feel that they're hurting the other guy. The producers in television are constantly saying that the directors just don't want to do it. In television it's a tough problem, because, for economic reasons, you've got to keep the good will of the producer.

●*JR:* Are there any formats you prefer? T.v. films or t.v. movies, specials, episodes?

●*BK:* Basically, I've been doing the long-forms, whether they are specials or evening-long programs. I did the first of the long, long-forms called *Vanished.* At four hours, it was the first television film made longer than two hours.

●*JR:* Because you had success there, or because you prefer it?

●*BK:* Well, it's a combination of both. For a television director it is more or less the ultimate format, because he has an opportunity to do things that have larger scope.

●*JR:* Do you really want to direct features, rather than television films?

●*BK:* I think that there are a number of reasons we all say we want to get into theatrical films—more time, more money, the opportunities for making more money are greater. In this town, our business is a very small one and it's very caste oriented. There's a great deal of snobbism involved; the motion picture people look down on the episode people; the hour people look down on the television people; the long-form people look down at the half-hour people. It's ridiculous; it's really ridiculous. Basically, the reasons so many want to get into theatrical films are numerous: the opportunity to do better things, to work with better people on a larger scope, to make more money; the success possibilities are greater, and also the opportunity to do the kind of material that one can't do on television.

●*JR:* There are approximately fifteen hundred members of the

Directors' Guild, three hundred of whom generally work. That speaks profoundly about direction, don't you think?

• *BK:* Many people who are members of our guild are really producers and actors who have, through the years, capriciously decided that they want to be directors. Burt Lancaster is a member of the Directors' Guild who doesn't work as a director, but he's a dues-paying member; he comes to all the meetings.

• *JR:* Do many actors use directing as a retirement home?

• *BK:* No, I don't think so. I think you have to understand that film is the director's medium. Even live television wasn't; on the stage it certainly isn't; but on film we have control so that we can turn a performance around in the cutting room, make it funny instead of sad. The director can say, "Let's do it again, until he gets the moment that he wants. He can then go into the editing room and cut it eighteen different ways; whereas, in live television or on the stage, the director can scream and order until the performance, but once the performance starts he cannot intrude. In live television we couldn't do it; certainly on the stage you can't.

• *JR:* I was told very vociferously by a group of actors that they believe the best directors were once actors.

• *BK:* That's a peculiar mystique attached to directing. The end result in anything is really the result, and not necessarily how you get to it. William Wyler, for example, one of the great directors of our time, never was able to be very articulate. He could often have an actor do something fifty and sixty times while not telling him what it was that he was looking for. But his greatness came from knowing when he got it. A lot of people don't. They are not capable of *doing,* you see. A man like Hitchcock, another example, does not work with actors; he thinks that if he casts them properly and if they are the kind of actors that he thinks they are, they should be able to do their own thing and leave him to the film techniques. As a result, he's absolutely a brilliant director. I think what those actors mean is that they're better able to relate to an ex-actor, and they can talk "motivations" and all that other nonsense.

I don't for a minute agree with that at all. There are some directors who are so articulate that they deserve medals for it. Then there are those who are inarticulate, like John Ford, who I think was one of the greatest motion picture directors, but he was an inarticulate man. You couldn't talk motivations with him; he would kick you in the ass.

I don't really watch too many other directors; I don't have the time, if nothing else. But I would guess that there are very few directors who work alike.

• *JR:* If you didn't get to watch many directors, how did you learn how to direct?

• *BK:* Basically, by running film. I learned by mistakes. I was very lucky. I was in New York when the whole new industry started, and none of the established people from motion pictures, radio, or the stage wanted to have anything to do with this stupid little medium that didn't pay anything—the network offices in New York, Philadelphia, and Washington. So they reached down to the bottom, where I was, and said, "You're a director." I was given the glorious opportunity to learn by mistakes, and I made plenty of them. We all did—still do—but in those days we all did. Out of that group came George Roy Hill and Delbert Mann and so on. We all started the same way; none of us really knowing what the hell it was all about. However, I think the best way to learn is to look at film. You can then see the technique. I must have seen John Ford's *The Quiet Man* eight times. I'll tell you something else; if I knew it was playing somewhere today, I'd go see it again.

• *JR:* What is your best television work?

• *BK:* Well, *Brian's Song* was unique. *Brian's Song,* I think, is the kind of material that comes once in a lifetime. For most people, maybe it never comes. It was a unique situation that generated the kind of attention that would never happen to me again, and I doubt it will happen too many more times in television.

• *JR:* Did you recognize it and its potential immediately?

• *BK:* No, I simply loved it. I am an ex-football player; I'm a sports nut; I knew Gale Sayers; I knew Brian Piccolo. The first time I read it I cried like a baby. None of us really foresaw its impact because we were all greatly concerned. It wasn't really a sports story, it was a love story—a love story between two men. There has been a syndrome in television and in motion pictures saying that sports don't work as a background because women are not interested in it. That had us concerned, but we recognized the possibilities of a very good thing. Life works in peculiar ways. I'll tell you one story about how these things seem to be almost foreordained: Before I came on the picture, the producer had hired an actor to play Gale Sayers—a very good actor, one of the best black actors around, but he was much older and bald. He was going to wear a toupee. And there it was. We left for Indiana on a Tuesday or Wednesday. The Saturday before, this actor was running in the sand at Malibu Beach and he popped his Achilles tendon. I received a call that night; he was in the hospital and they were operating on him. I had arranged with the casting director to see a group of other actors on Monday; we had to make a decision on Monday night because I was leaving Tuesday for the location. In came a bunch of actors; I had just about made up my mind to use George Stafford Brown, an excellent actor. We had been at it all day, and I was getting tired. It was 5 o'clock and I said, "Look, let's hire George Brown. I think he will be fine." The casting director said, "Well, I've one more guy who's driving in from Malibu." In came Billy Williams, whom I did not know. The weirdest part of the situation was that when we got to Indiana, Gale was there, and Billy came out in his blue blazer and Kansas tie. They stood talking to each other, and it was as though they were twins. Now, I had no idea of that resemblance. I wish I could tell you that I was that brilliant. I had no idea that they were going to look alike.

•*JR:* What should a director have to say about things like content and conditions of broadcast?

•*BK:* Well, we're all realists. I think we all recognize that we work in a monopoly situation: networks that control the televiewing of our country. Directors know that there's nothing we're going to do about that situation. In so far as controlling content is concerned, we're all desperately concerned about it.

We live in a violent world; it's awful what's going on out there. Every facet of art, every facet of entertainment reflects that violence, and we'd like to turn it around. However, audiences won't watch it if it's not there. Every day I get the ratings, and I see that we had a show like *Crackup on Highway 42,* a horrible thing. I don't know what to do about that.

•*JR:* I've had producers tell me, "Now, what the hell do you expect us to do? ACT, the FCC and the networks tell us the programs are too violent, too sexual, maybe obscene to some people. We've got to cut it down." At the same time, the shows that are relatively more violent, more obscene or more sexual have larger audiences. Now something's wrong.

• *BK:* When you give them something else, they just don't watch it. Character studies go down the hole. It's one of those ironies that I guess are insoluble. It's very disturbing. And I have to tell you that there's nothing gratuitous about it at all. Many, many, many of us are deeply concerned, but we can't fight it because the numbers prove us wrong all the time. This is a commercial business in which numbers mean something. It's a miserable problem.

• *JR:* What's the process by which you direct?

• *BK:* The biggest problem is getting the time to rehearse. There's no use rehearsing for just a day or two. That doesn't do anything. It just opens up questions that you can't answer. If one had two or three weeks, it would make sense, but if somebody says you've got a day to rehearse, I'd say, "Thank you, I'm not interested."

I try to have long discussions with the actors beforehand so I can attempt to lay out the characters and the story. Generally that will do until I get on the stage. Then I attempt to rehearse a scene thoroughly before I start breaking it up and filming it: from movement to movement and so on. Then I rehearse as much as I can while the scene is being lit. There's a school of thought that says that motion picture acting, television acting is not really acting. It's improvisation. It's a different kind of thing from stage acting altogether. This is the way I feel. You can't act until you really have devoted a great deal of time and thought and worry to working out the kinks. Then you can really have something. With improvisation you're likely to get a kind of freshness, a kind of discovery that's interesting and can make sense. That's what I attempt to do.

It's wrong to try to say that motion picture acting is really "acting" as we know it. It isn't. In the days of live television, we often rehearsed for three and a half weeks, and we all thought that wasn't enough. At least we could see a beginning, a middle, and an end—and we could try to smooth out the wrinkles.

Today, we just don't have that luxury. There is no way that a person can act a part, perform, find a character without having the time for the stuff to sink in.

• *JR:* Does this force you, then, to search for types when you're casting?

• *BK:* Well, we all search for types, even in the theater. No question about that. There is a reason. Spencer Tracy always gave a certain kind of performance. If that's what you thought a character required then you cast Spencer Tracy. By the way, directors are type-cast too; cameramen and others are type-cast, because the director does not have the freedom to explore.

• *JR:* Do you think anything like the *Auteur* theory exists in television direction? Can you go in and watch a television tape and say, "Oh, that's Franklin Shaffner?"

• *BK:* I don't think so.

• *JR:* Do most of the more successful directors direct both in television and in films, or just in one or the other?

• *BK:* Some do. Some go between. I've gone between. When they go to theatrical films, they usually stay.

• *JR:* Other directors have remarked that they don't watch much television.

• *BK:* Well, I do. I was born and raised in television. Television is my life. I watch it.

• *JR:* What do you think directors ought to be doing that they aren't?

• *BK:* It's hard to say. I'm on the board of the Directors' Guild and I used to be a member of Television Arts and Sciences. I resigned five years ago because I felt they were only concerned with the awards show, and I told them that. The year that they say we're not going to give an award at all this year because nothing was good enough is the year I'll come back. After all these years the Directors' Guild has put together a Speakers Bureau; we're actually taping some of our old-time guys. Everybody seems to have to learn everything all over again on his own. We seldom get together as directors to discuss mutual problems, mutual techniques, new ways. It's always been very, very disturbing to me. I can't think of an industry of this size that doesn't attempt to perpetuate itself. Management people come and go. Nobody seems to get any training to be anything. Besides that, we don't even talk amongst ourselves. In Russia, they do this. We need an organization that discusses how we can make our art, or our business, or whatever you want to call it, better. How can we better it? What can we do to leave something of some value behind? It's very disturbing to me.

• *JR:* Maybe this touches on the same thing: What do you see as the major problems facing television?

• *BK:* Well, I think the biggest concern is that television is grinding things out like a big sausage grinder. I was told in my early days that there are only so many stories, so many plots. I worry about the formulization of everything. I think you can almost tell by a watch where a program is and what's going to happen. I don't know where all the new material is going to come from. I really don't.

Employment is another issue: We're not in the manufacturing business; we don't make shoes. We can't have steady employment. Show business is a very ephemeral, whipped creamy kind of thing. And what we have to sell is very whipped creamy. I don't really believe that most people know what a director is and what he does. Even the people who are critics and people in our industry don't really know. You see, it's almost impossible in my opinion for someone to see something—either on the big screen, on the stage, or at home—and say, "Hey, that's a great piece of direction." Direction is a combination of three basic elements, at the very least: a writer, an actor, and a director. Who knows, unless you were there when the thing occurred, what's good direction and what isn't?

• *JR:* Most of these areas—acting, direction and production—are closed clubs?

• *BK:* You ask young Steve Spielberg; he'll tell you how he got in. It was as much a closed corporation when he started, and he came out of Cal. State L.A.—not Yale, or Columbia, but Cal. State—not Yale School of Drama, not UCLA but Cal. State, Long Beach. I don't know how these things occur, but they occur. I do believe that if you have the ability, somewhere along the line you'll get a chance. I really believe that.

• *JR:* You sound like a mystic.

• *BK:* Okay. Years ago I was a substitute for a friend who was teaching a class in advanced directing at UCLA to a group of

twelve young men and women. They called one day and said
that they wanted to come down to see me. It was their thought
that when a person got a degree in directing or a degree in theater arts he should automatically be taken into the Directors'
Guild as an assistant director, at the very least. What was I to say?
Here were people who had devoted four years of their time, effort,
and money. It just doesn't work that way. We do have a trainee
program. It's awful, because we take so few, six a year. It's
disgraceful. However, it's been one of the most successful things
that we've ever done, because everybody who's been through the
program has turned out to be terrific. It was a struggle to get it to
six, because we are faced with a long list of assistant directors,
many of them out of work much of the year. They say, "Hey, I've
been a member of this organization. I've been paying dues all
these years, and you're bringing young kids in to take the bread
out of my mouth?" How do you answer that?

• *JR:* What is government's role in television?

• *BK:* I do not think that we have policed ourselves as well as
we should have. And I think that the family hour is an attempt at
self-regulation. I think that whatever experience we have with
PBS is just a monumental headache. It's committee on committee. It's really to the point where it becomes hopeless. It is hopeless to deal with them. However, I do not believe that anybody
should turn on their set in the morning and leave it on till two in
the next morning. There's such a thing as selectivity, and I think
we have to select. If we could see one thing a night that's worthwhile, it would be terrific. I watch PBS all the time. I think I must
watch that channel more than I even watch the other stations.
You know, I have great affection and respect for it, but it
embodies a certain kind of problem that's rather unique. At the
Corporation for Public Broadcasting, there are ten other people
who say, "No, you shouldn't do that," or "You should do this."
As long as *they* make the decisions, it's a problem. Commercial
organizations find it difficult to deal with.

• *JR:* Anything about television that I've missed?

• *BK:* I would say that there is a basic way to make a shoe. You
know, there's a last, and nails, and hammers. If you make shoes,
you can make one and show your wares. We can't. There is no-

body who can predict success. In direction, there is really no one way to achieve the best result. There are some people who do it by screaming, there are others who do it by total silence; there are other people who, like William Wyler, say "Do it again"; other people who will talk you into the ground. They all work for one director or another. I was taught, as an example, that if you saw the direction, it was bad direction. I was taught that the *play's* the thing. I was taught that if you could see the acting, it was poor, because it has taken you away from what it's all about, the story. I firmly believe in this. I firmly believe that all of us have our own peculiar ways of directing but it's the end result that counts.

Daniel Petrie

Like several of the directors interviewed, Petrie was first attracted to acting on the college stage. He worked as a professional actor after his college career. Later, he directed the features Lifeguard, The Idol, Raisin in the Sun, *and* The Bramble Bush. *He directed television series for most of the production units in Hollywood during the 1960s. Today, he works almost exclusively in long-form productions.*

Television: Sybil; Eleanor and Franklin [I & II]; *and* Silent Night, Lonely Night.

• *Dan Petrie:* Tape production is much like the old days of live television; you move faster, indeed over longer hours, so it makes it very, very exhausting. That's why, in spite of the fact that I've had a couple of very good outings with television in the last few years, I'm anxious to get out of t.v.

• *John Ravage:* It's a comment I hear over and over again.

• *DP:* It's one of the most common comments of all. They want feature production quality and at the same time they want it on Tuesday—"they" being the networks or whatever production agency you're working with. It's "they" who control.

• *JR:* Are there production differences, are there personnel differences between t.v. and films?

• *DP:* Not really, no. There are very, very good people who are doing the longer forms. Top people who've worked in features all the time. I worked last with a chap by the name of Mario Tozzi; he was the cameraman on *Sybil*. Right after that he did *MacArthur*, and just before that he'd done *Report to the Commissioner* and *Hearts of the West*. He'd just done those, and indeed he had done a feature with me earlier, so I was acquainted with him personally as well as with his work. He was doing television.

● *JR:* Do you consciously think any differently when you're filming for television?

● *DP:* Not consciously, but I think unconsciously I do. If you, in the morning, have a schedule to meet for that particular day of, say, six pages, then when you start setting up shots for that particular day, you're going to make certain compromises that you might not otherwise make. You might want to do a long and very, very interesting master if you were doing a feature—where you would only do two pages a day. However, I don't think at that point it's a conscious process. It's almost unconscious.

● *JR:* Shifting gears?

● *DP:* Yes. If you have a deadline whereby you have to get grades out to your students and you have forty papers to read by Friday of this week, you would in all conscience work at them. But if you had twenty papers to do, your input on those papers probably would be a little bit better, a little bit more thorough than it would be with the forty. And it's exactly the same thing in my occupation. But consciously I don't think, "I'm going to slough off." Not at all. You're going to give them every bit of your best; at the same time you're conscious of the fact that if I give two hours to one paper, I'm not going to get my work done. In television, however—as opposed to features—you don't have the kind of properties that some of the more interesting specials will allow you to do. For example, *Eleanor and Franklin* would never have been done as a feature film. It's not exactly a commercial notion. It turned out to be very commercial and highly satisfactory to the sponsor. Their message was heard by a great many people.

● *JR:* How do you account for the fact that there is an audience for this kind of material?

● *DP: Sybil* was a best-selling book, and it stayed in that category for a number of years. There was a great deal of interest in that particular story, so it was highly promotable. As a matter of fact, our best commercials for viewership of the following week were done in the course of the screening of *Gone with the Wind,* which was the highest-rated film ever put on t.v. In the case of *Eleanor and Franklin,* even though the book was not a best-seller, it did very well. They were two rather fascinating characters in our history.

We were able to hike the rating by an appeal to schools. In Philadelphia, the Philadelphia *Enquirer* in its Sunday edition printed the entire script in a separate section, and that went to every reader of the paper. Also, school children were asked by teachers to read that script. It was a program in readership. The results of the plan were reported by John O'Connor in the *New York Times;* the reading level in the Philadelphia schools on the basis of that one project went up one year. It's really incredible.

- *JR:* Do you like seeing something that's a piece of yourself used for the utilitarian purpose of ratings?

- *DP:* I think it's great. I love it. My original bent as a young adult was to be a do-gooder, to be a teacher. I went to Columbia University and I got my master's in Adult Education. My idea was to go back to my little college town in Nova Scotia and be the educational director of a radio station.

- *JR:* Most of the directors I've talked to tend to be actors or technicians.

- *DP:* I became an actor while I was studying for my master's at Columbia. I ended up in a producer's office who was casting a Broadway play, and I got the part. So, we went out of town and opened in Philadelphia, played about ten performances there, came to Broadway and played one hundred and ten performances. That got me: "How are you going to keep them down on the farm after they've seen Broadway?" So it was a natural jump to doing other plays as an actor. I did the road company of *I Remember Mama,* and then I did an off-Broadway show in New York as an actor. Ended up in the road company of *I Remember Mama* in Chicago. Then I decided I really didn't know anything about acting—even though I was doing it—so I decided to go to Northwestern and work on my Ph.D. and to study drama. When I applied to take acting courses, they asked what was my background. I told them well I was appearing right then at the Studebaker Theatre, and they could come and see some of my background. Well, the head of the department had seen it; he was very impressed, and he offered me a job as a graduate assistant, teaching acting. I said, "No, that's not the idea, I want to *take* acting," but he insisted. That's the way I learned acting—by *teaching*, as opposed to *taking*. It was a good way; I just kept a chapter ahead in Stanislavsky.

Acting is a skill like anything else; it can be taught. I think I had a natural bent for it anyway, and I enjoyed it. In teaching acting you are, in effect, directing; I began to like that idea. That was something I never thought of myself as doing.

I went out to teach at Creighton University in Omaha, Nebraska. I became so immersed in all of the activities—not only the teaching activities. Creighton had WOW-TV on campus, but WOW-TV had not yet built its building. That became my toy. Between teaching classes and working with that equipment, it was really Christmas. I discovered that I didn't like teaching all that much—possibly because of where the teaching was being done. At Creighton I was teaching pharmacy students "Speech 1" and "Public Speaking 1," which were requirements for graduation. They were highly unmotivated. When I was a graduate at Northwestern all of my kids were very highly motivated. They were all acting buffs, and it was really a great pleasure. So I said to myself, "I've got to get out of here." I went to Chicago and pleaded with a guy at NBC to give me a job to save my sanity. He said, "Well, I can't do it until mid-January." I said, "That's too late; the second semester will have started." I went back to Omaha empty-handed, but the day after I got back he called and said, "When can you get here?" I said, "When do you need me?" He said, "Yesterday." "I'll be there at the end of the week." That ended my academic career.

• *JR:* You made the comment that one of the reasons *Sybil* and *Franklin and Eleanor* were popular was that they came from famous books; they had some prior visibility. We know that the television audience is not a reading audience. How can you say that they would have been attracted by what they probably weren't even aware existed?

- *DP:* They may not have read the book, but they read the title, or they heard it discussed. The paperback of *Sybil* sold over a million copies. I'm sure it helped the promotion because it was a very, very special story.

- *JR:* The types of films that you have done indicate an interest in public television; have you ever worked with PBS?

- *DP:* I did one last January or February. I did *Harry Truman, Plain Speaking.*

- *JR:* What do you think is the potential of public television? I say "potential" because nothing much has been realized in many parts of the country.

- *DP:* I suppose so. Here you hear about it a great deal.

- *JR:* Some directors say that's where I go to wash the business out of my head. Other people say that PBS is so screwed up they wouldn't go back there for beans. There seem to be very strong feelings about PBS among directors. I wonder if you've run across that?

- *DP:* I had a delightful experience working in public television. The program manager of KQED called me just recently to ask if I would do another program for them. I even entertained the idea for about a week and a half, and then I realized that I just wouldn't have time. But it was not a matter of not wanting to do it; I would have loved to have worked with them again. I thought the station was a good operation, and they work like beavers. One of the problems, it seems, with public television is its place on the dial. Public television is usually UHF in most parts of the country, and most sets are not very good at receiving UHF. It's impossible to tune and people are turned off; it's just cumbersome. That's what's really wrong with it: lack of accessibility. We have a marvelous station here, of course, and it's right in the middle of our dial, channel 6. The picture is absolutely wonderful; they call it channel 28 but where you get it on your dial is on this number 6. Maybe you have to have the cable, I don't know.

- *JR:* Okay, you just answered it. Yes, you do have to have cable. It seems to me that is the problem most places. Only certain people are ever going to be able to afford cable because it is a luxury to have a cable.

- *DP:* We pay $9.95 a month for that cable.

• *JR:* Have you done much in electronic television?

• *DP:* I started in live television; it has no terror for me. For many people it's a step forward, a step into a new thing. For me, it's a step backward, a thing I grew up with. The new editing techniques are much more sophisticated, of course. One of the things that bothers me about the editing techniques is that you start with all of your information from whatever cameras that you used, and you build that onto a master. "Okay now we take two of B up to this frame. Zip, put that on. Now we'll take one of C. Now we go to A again. We take four and we'll put it here." You build it all the way. Toward the end of that tape, you say, "My God, that stuff that he said in the first ten minutes of the show was all repeated and we really don't need it." Back to square one. We're going to have to do that again, because you can't just nip that out of the middle. That's a tremendous drawback for me. The film is more flexible in spite of the fact that it is so much more time consuming. The editorial process becomes such a creative part of the whole. My imagination stops short of what the future ramifications could be; tape is limited to me. One of the ironic things is that when I will finish with *Eleanor and Franklin* on film, we'll transfer that to tape. Some producers won't do it, won't go along with that. They insist that there is a lost quality in the transfer. I transferred the last *Eleanor and Franklin* and stayed there on every shot. I also "helped" it a little by changing certain shots that I felt were a little too light, a little too dark. I felt I was able to help it a little bit. Video doesn't have subtleties; it can't store as much information as film. That seems to be such a bold statement, yet I've found very few people who have actually tested it.

Evidently there is a certain kind of lag in the electronics dealing with lights and darks. They explained that to me in the transfer process. Evidently, the electronic equipment searches out the black and almost rejects the light, so that there is a differential there. On film you can get a real, hard black. On t.v. there is a question about that.

• *JR:* What do you see as the biggest problems facing directors who want to work in television?

• *DP:* It's really a very good question, and of course because it is good, it's difficult to answer. The public, unfortunately, is dictating to a great extent what goes on in television. A lot of people disagree with that theory. They say the ratings really don't indicate the successes like *Eleanor and Franklin*. They also say that this is an indication that the public doesn't want *Laverne and Shirley* every week. But as long as the ratings are believed by sponsors, the public is dictating what goes on.

●*JR:* Is that wrong?

●*DP:* Well, no I don't think it is wrong, but for people who want to do something other than *Joe Forrester* or *Marcus Welby, M.D.,* and *Medical Center,* it is very difficult. You can't choose to work on anything other than what is there.

A lot of fellows who were my peers are still working in episodic television; I run into them every now and then and they say, "Oh man, you're so lucky that you broke through." They say, "We're still dealing in that kind of junk." And it does get terribly enervating after a while because the shows do have a pattern to them: that second act dire circumstance that the leading character is put into and then the sequence in which you have to solve the problem through action. You know them after a while by heart. It's really, really painful. You may come in as a new director and say, "I'd like to try a little experiment with your show." They all welcome it tremendously; they all say, "Hey, that's great, man. A little fresh blood." The very first day that you go in, fear takes over on the part of the actors. "That's against my character," or "My character wouldn't work that way." They know what was successful for them—has been successful for two years. So, no sir, they do not really want to experiment with anything that would change the image that they have been presenting.

●*JR:* In essence, the actor has really the first cut.

●*DP:* Oh yes, exactly, exactly. If you have to do eight pages in a particular day, you begin with a whole different mind set than you would if you were going to shoot four or two. You are also dealing with an actor who has grooved himself or been grooved by somebody else; it allows you very little sort of self-expression, if you will.

The value, of course, is that this experience allowed me to be on the sound stage for almost nine months of any given year. I was on the sound stage constantly, dealing with all of the problems that you encounter on a sound stage. After a while you begin to know whether it worked or it didn't work. So, you're not likely to make that experiment again if it didn't work. As an area in which you would want to work for year in and year out, however, it's not too good.

•*JR:* It just occurred to me that there's a kind of sociological function that a t.v. director has that other directors don't— hugging, back patting, kissing. Is it absolutely necessary in order to achieve results?

•*DP:* A great deal of ego-hype goes on in those things. I imagine if a director couldn't do that he wouldn't be successful. It's very, very much a part of the stock and trade that he must pay lip service to that kind of thing. It does help those actors, you know, to feel that they're obviously adored not just for what they do but for who they are.

•*JR:* It puts a new dimension on the term "actor."

I've heard directors, especially in situation comedy, tell me that there's no sense in trying to tell an actor how to be that character. "He has been that character longer than anybody on earth. Therefore, I don't even concern myself with that." And it seems to me that the person who is saying that is saying, "I'm abrogating part of my responsibility. I'm just going to do other things: I'm going to arrange the camera; I'm going to set up the shots; I'm going to move them through their positions." He reduces direction to cinematography.

•*DP:* Well, as I told you before, I found that out the hard way by coming up against so many actors who at first welcomed my appearance. Oh, they knew that I was an actor. Immediately I became regarded as a threat, and I wouldn't get a good performance from them, if I insisted on my interpretations. So the better part of valor was to say, "No, no, no. What you're doing is great, just great!" Then I would try for something else, not exactly cinematography, I suppose, to find a visual equivalent of what I saw in that character.

Noam Pitlik

Pitlik exemplifies a different generation from most of the successful directors in television. His career began with under-

graduate theater at Temple University in Philadelphia and included a Master's Degree from New York University, also in theater. After studying acting with Paul Mann and Uta Hagen he began an acting career in both New York and Los Angeles. In addition, he appeared as an actor in eighteen features and a large number of television series.

In 1973 he began directing for television. As of January 1978, he was a staple of the Barney Miller *series, having directed over thirty-five episodes.*

Television series: The New Dick Van Dyke Show; The Practice; Phyllis; The Betty White Show; On Our Own; Holmes and Yoyo: Alice; *and* Fish.

● *John Ravage:* What is it that makes a television director?

● *Noam Pitlik:* Well, I think that each medium has its own set of techniques. On the stage, it's one problem, whereas in a mechanical medium like film or television, it's another. Except to the degree that those differ, directing is the same job. You have, in the film and television, the luxury of guaranteeing that the audience is going to be looking at a certain place, which you don't have on stage. What you do on stage is try to make sure they are looking there. They have the option not to. Part of the job is to make sure they are looking at Hamlet and not the corpse. To that degree it's the same. The technical differences I consider not minor but of a secondary nature.

The thing that's common to all of it is the need to deal with a certain piece of material and a certain group of people—actors, writers, directors, and producers. Whether it's on a stage or on a piece of film or a tape, that's the crux of the whole thing; that's why everybody is there.

● *JR:* Do you approach a new assignment with a predetermined attitude toward how you are going to handle or manipulate the actors? I've noticed that you seem to be more involved in the process of character delineation, line reading, pacing, everything, than anybody I've seen so far.

● *NP:* It seems that the major function of the job is to make the piece work. And in the end, it's the actors who are going to have to do that. I mean there's a point in television at which there are no more rewriters, you know. It may be the minute before the performance, but there is a point at which you are not going to correct anything on a typewriter any more and it leaves the actors in the position of having to do that. One of the directorial functions is to help them get to the point where they can do that. I think that a large part is values or time. My attitude is that if you can make the material work and if the actors are working, they can handle any change that comes. If there is some tenuousness about what they are doing, what this moment is or that moment is, then changes throw them altogether. But once they are working and once they are working together, then you say, "Instead of doing it over here, because I can't cover it, play it over there." Once the scene is working and the place is not inappropriate, you can deal with all of the technical problems that happen when you try to put it on camera. There are shots you just can't get unless a guy is so and so and so . . .

This situation of *Barney Miller* is unique. In my experience almost never is there a complete script to work with. The first show of the season, I think, had a complete script. It was interesting for me since most of the directing that I've done has been on *Barney Miller*. I learned that there really is a little more time than you think; there's less time than you'd like but more time than you think if you take the time to make it better. What's the reality of this situation? Why don't we try something else? You get an idea, you try it.

Of all the theatrical media, the collaborative aspect of television is most marked. In a feature picture, a director can have a concept, and he can also have a need to shoot two and a half pages a day so that he can have the time to mold everybody into a preconception that he has. Here you are more dependent on all the other contributors. In the case of this show, I get the script at the same time the actors do so I can't sit down ahead of time and figure it out. I don't have the time to sit down. Maybe it wouldn't be as good anyhow, I don't know. So it becomes a kind of mix of ideas that everybody throws in. You see something out of that sense of freedom to be able to try anything. You see something that's better than anything you might have thought of anyhow, and also it keeps a certain liveliness going which is important for everybody. It doesn't become rote, where the actor walks in and says "Oh yeah I know I'm this kind of character." It makes for better work all around, and it makes for the use of everybody's best qualities. Includes people on crews, too. If a cameraman says to me, "There is something wrong with this shot; I don't like it," then my feeling is to say, "Well, what do you have in mind?" I've worked with this crew so long that it happens often. It isn't a formal thing. I'll say, "Such and such a shot," and the cameraman will say, "I don't think we should do it," which is terrific. I would think this holds for directors anywhere. One of the major functions of the job is to get the best or to have all these people operating at their best levels.

● *JR:* To get the best product you can?

● *NP:* Yes, but it comes from the best work of each of the individuals. I found out about all of this at a time when I wasn't consciously seeking to be a director. The first time I ever saw all this clearly was in a picture I did as an actor, which Billy Wilder was directing. He would accept an idea from anybody, and these guys who had worked with him on crews for years would walk up to him and say, "Wouldn't it be funny if . . . ?" and sometimes it *was.* He would do it, even for me, walking in as an actor. I got an acting job from him when I came on a set and read. I said, "Bill," I probably said, "Mr. Wilder," I have two ideas about how to approach this. I explained them to him, and he listened very carefully, but did not give me an answer right away. Two hours later, he discussed it with me again, but he had thought about it. It wasn't "You, know, I have my notion and that's it." Because my feeling was this way he was talking about doing it so and so. It was clear that he accepted the input and was deciding on the basis of his judgment. That atmosphere on a set is terrific and makes it fun in what otherwise could be a grind.

● *JR:* Nonetheless there are very serious restrictions and frustrations placed upon a television director. For instance, the role of Nielsen ratings, the role of the networks, the role of the executive producers—your inability to fire an actor who is lousy.

● *NP:* What you are talking about is what virtually everybody I know in this business wants. You are talking about *control.* Unless you're Billy Wilder or Hitchcock or Richard Lester, or not a great many directors when you count them—unless you *are* one of those guys, you only get the first cut. Unless you negotiate.

There is no question that Billy Wilder cuts his own picture; the product is his doing. And in picture making, whether it's on tape or film, that's really the ultimate control of the product. Dealing with this reality is one of the emotional problems that you have to adjust to, to accept the reality of the situation. I don't have the power. In the end, Danny cuts *Barney Miller*. It's his show.

• *JR:* The network is on his back too. . . .

• *NP:* Actually, all the network can say is that you can't say *this* or you can't say *that* or "We don't want you to do that story." The director can fight them, and he can gamble his money in fighting them. But the ultimate power that the network has is that they won't air it. When you've got a successful show, however, they use their power less stridently than they might with a less popular one. So, while that is the ultimate power, it isn't really used all that often. It becomes a big headline when NBC or CBS cancels a program because it's too controversial.

In other words, Norman Lear made *Mary Hartman, Mary Hartman* and took a chance. Whatever happens as a result, the network doesn't control it. It may control what the public sees, but it doesn't control what will be made.

But all that doesn't affect me very much and it's not my concern. I'm not going to direct somebody to drop their pants, because I obviously know that isn't going to get on. The attitude that I have about it is that I am doing my job, and I do it to the best of my ability for as long as I can—and then my job is over. That's the reality of it. Listen, I'd love to be in the position of power that we were talking about a minute ago. If I were in that position, I wouldn't have the problem of dealing with reality—I'd have a different one. Until you're the boss, you're not the boss.

• *JR:* And the conditions are clear?

• *NP:* Very clear. At each place you direct you also have different levels of success. Danny Arnold is probably more involved in all the aspects of the production of *Barney Miller* than any executive producer.

• *JR:* That brings up an analogous question: What is a good television director? Is he merely a good guy who will tolerate the system?

• *NP:* No. The question you just raised is immaterial in the same way that how we deal with producers and networks is immaterial to being a good director. Those questions may pertain to how you get through a week—which may make you better or worse at your job. The job is a simply stated one: bring together all the elements of a script, acting, staging, and the physical element necessary to a picture in such a way that it fulfills its purpose relative to an audience. If it's a comedy, hopefully you will make an audience laugh. If you succeed in doing that, honestly within the framework of the reality of what you're doing, then you are doing a good job. For example, if the only way you could get a laugh is by having Barney trip over a chair . . . you're cheating. There are scripts that call for that, but the script defines everything. The characters define that. Writers sometimes cheat on that more than anybody; they will make a fool of somebody in order to get a laugh when that person is not a fool.

● *JR:* They can't think of anything else.

● *NP:* That's exactly right. You can do that directorially too; you can't think of anything to do, and then you throw things. That's when people laugh. So then, the framework of the reality of the situation is established within the material. When it's a television series, the actors have a very strong sense of the reality of what their characters are doing. In *M*A*S*H* those guys are doctors in an emergency hospital on the front lines of a war. They engage in their activity and the comedy comes out of the characters and the situations they are placed in. The same is true of *Barney Miller:* being faithful to this reality—while making sure that the script is also faithful to it. So you don't use joke props, and you don't use strange behavior and loud noises just to get the laughs. If you can do that, then you are doing your job. The style is then determined by the material and the nature of the piece. It is sometimes impossible.

Holmes and Yoyo was merely *Holmes and Yoyo.* I did one of those, and it was very hard to bring the same standards to bear because, ultimately, you are dependent upon what's on the page. I don't think any director ever made a great picture out of bad material. He may have made it look good; he may have made it exciting to watch, but he never made it a great picture. It is, then, the center of the responsibility and work that you have to do. Being faithful to that is the crux of the matter.

• *JR:* You mentioned a while ago that you sought to make the material work for a particular audience. Who is your audience, the audience to whom you play the material?

• *NP:* Me. I find it very difficult to try to imagine what will make twenty million people laugh. I don't know the answer to that. I don't know how to determine that. If I tried to figure out what they would laugh at . . . I don't know how to do that. Sometimes, you know that they'll laugh, but the only thing that I can truly rely on is my own taste. If an actor does something that makes me laugh, then my tendency is to not change it. If I think that there is supposed to be a laugh—and the actor doesn't make me laugh—then I try to find a way to amuse myself. I try to find a way to communicate to him the humor that I see in what is written.

I've tried other ways. I've tried to work a whole show with stuff that I only laughed at twice during the whole week. I knew what we were doing; it's just not going to make me laugh. I can still direct that, because it's clear what the intention is and it's possible to do it. The most fun is when the writing is good enough to preclude the cheap shot and the falling down, etc.—to make it work in other ways. If the crap makes me laugh, then I really feel terrific. There's a certain self-deception that sometimes pertains— this also may be a partial answer to an earlier question—to the nature of how we do this business under the pressure of time and money and all those other things. There is for actors and directors a susceptibility to the suspension of our own disbelief. While we're doing something we may see greater merit in it than when we look at it later. It's a necessary trick of mind that enables us to avoid saying, "I'm not going to do this shit. Get out of here, fella." Obviously, there are scripts on every show that are so bad that I would like to avoid them. "What am I doing this for?"

• *JR:* You have two sequences in this show, one an opening telephone conversation with Yemana and another between the doctor and Wojohowicz that the actors don't like and do not understand, as actors. They don't care for their lines. How do you approach that situation?

• *NP:* It's an interesting question. It's one of the central problems of directing series television. The problem with that opening piece has to do with a certain actor's sense of security, which is in the toilet. There's only so much that you can do about that. I can't get in his skin and tell him to change. I spent an inordinate amount of time thinking over just these bits, trying to convince him that what was there was good. To this moment he has never done it. Not yet. Eventually he will—because at that moment when an actor knows there is an audience present, at that moment something is going to happen to overcome his unconscious insecurities and his sense that his function in this series is not what he wishes. Then he'll probably come up with it all. [The sequence was deleted by the producer in final editing.] I'm relying upon a switch that gets thrown so that an actor has to put aside the game and do the work. As long as it's rehearsal, not the real thing, there's no way you can make him do it unless he wants to. He starts to want to do it when it is going to be permanent. It is one of the most difficult and recurrent of problems in series television. The emotional aspect of not being the star—when everybody wants to be—is even harder for actors to deal with than for other people in differing professions.

Even with the limitation that I have placed upon me, my job requires that I operate at a certain level of responsibility and authority. Actors function in even more of an inferior position. I can tell an actor—I really hardly ever *tell*, as a matter of fact— that there is a point at which he or she has to join the process. There's no way I can force him to do it. Those intricacies of personal relationships and psychological states of actors under given circumstances are often very difficult to deal with. The understanding that they're there can be very fruitful. Having been an actor, I can sympathize very strongly with that situation. That's why I became a director. I was tired of that shit. I was not getting to play the things that I wanted. That sense of frustration was going to lead to some change in my life. It all can be insurmountable to some actors.

In the case of the scene between the doctor and Wojo, what has unfortunately happened is that there was a piece of miscasting— an unavoidable part of series television. Not to say that I have not miscast characters myself. Very often because of the nature of a director's schedule and the production schedule, a director does not get involved in casting. He is presented by the producer with a number of actors who he has never met before. In this show I do not know any of the guest performers; I've never worked with them. And there is a case of one of them being seriously miscast in a pivotal role. Specifically, when Danny cast her, he made the decision to use her in this show. I could not be involved in that decision because I was not around. He helped create a great part of this monster. Not having been there during the formative process, the producer may come in to look at the results—when maybe he should work with that result instead of trying to alter the character at a later point—all of which is going to make things worse. Since I was not involved in the casting, the problem has grown to its present state. If the producer imposes an interpretation upon an actor—even if the director does not agree—the director cannot change it or say, "No, he didn't mean that."

• *JR:* This must happen all the time.

• *NP:* No, not all of the time. As you can see from the cast of *Barney Miller,* Danny Arnold can be absolutely masterful in casting. His choice of actors, acting styles, settings, everything... it's a truly sensational cast. When these conflicts happen, I accommodate to the limits of my ability.

Let's say there is a situation in which the producer is not like Danny. If a performer is miscast and has a limited craft—I try to find what he can do best, and then I just leave it alone, try to keep whatever I can as clean as possible. The job has to get done; there are no extensions after the last shooting day. There are cases in which the performer is fired. That's happened on this show and others. It is certainly the most efficient way to solve those problems. However, that cannot be done on the last two days of shooting. These problems are not, however; unique to television directing. If you want to, you can go back and retake something, the same as in features. The difference is that you have a very limited amount of time, and this may produce more mistakes that you don't have a chance to rectify in the process. You learn to live with it a great deal in television.

• *JR:* Do you find that putting up with it all—the actors, the producers, and the writers—is a predominant sentiment in television directing?

• *NP:* Yes, there's a lot of that. I've been lucky in that I don't feel put upon or have to take a lot of that. I've heard warnings about some producers that I've started to work with, but it has often turned out that they were not like their reviews. They may be like that, surely, but whatever relationship I evolved with them was different. In a situation where you develop a long-term relationship, like mine here with Danny Thomas' *The Practice*, there have been confrontations at times between me and regular members of the company. In those actions, I have had to say, "If this is the way it's going to be, then I won't do the show." Not that that was any great threat to anyone. In the evolution of my relationships with these people, things did change. It was good for me.

- *JR:* Did you leave or stay, on that particular episode?
- *NP:* I stayed. I stayed under modified circumstances.
- *JR:* I remember Paul Bogart's saying that the day he walked off a show because he would not tolerate a certain actor or producer was the most fearful day of his professional life. He went home thinking that the telephone might never ring for his services again. It rang after two days. He said he had found a new way to conduct himself as a director.
- *NP:* My attitude is a little more moderate. I have rarely felt that the problems could be easily resolved by my putting my "directorial self" against one other person, "It's him or me," so to speak. The object always has to be to get the program done. If the show can be done, then there's no reason that anybody cannot work with anybody. We're all committed to that end. Television is television, as far as quality is concerned. You may work on two scripts a year that you think are really good.

I enjoy this kind of work. I want to do it, insofar as it's possible. I know that I do not have the ultimate control and that I'm not going to get it by walking out. I did however, confront a producer in post-production—one whose personality I had not correctly perceived—and suggested that the program be cancelled or the show recast. Still, I didn't walk out. I walked out of a cutting room once, but I came back in later.

- *JR:* You have worked with actors who have distinctly different personalities and acting approaches. Some come from a theatrical background, others out of nightclub comedy.
- *NP:* Again, these actors are good—at their *best*—when they're real. Their honesty to their characters is what sets them off. In both shows the lead actors play their character like actors, not

like comedians. In effect, my job is the same. The actors and their approaches may change, but my job is still to get the reality of their performances.

• *JR:* But doesn't the actor have the ultimate choice? After all, he is the one performing.

• *NP:* Not really. No one may ever see the characterization if the producer doesn't like what has been done. This is the great fear of all actors when something new is being tried: it may get cut out. The differences that you mention are really ones of personality.

• *JR:* What do you view as the major problems facing you as a director?

• *NP:* Besides working itself, you mean?

• *JR:* Besides that.

• *NP:* Material. Getting good scripts. This business ought to be great fun. The two things that keep it from being so, when it's not, are difficult mixes of personalities and bad material. The latter is the hardest thing to work on. That five days seems like months, often. When you're bored by Wednesday, and shooting goes until Friday, it's like Saturday will never come. The business aspect of television is also aggravating. I find that I'm much more stringently type-cast as a director than I ever was as an actor. I'm a "multiple-camera comedy man." I finally got to do a single-camera show this year, and it was a big struggle to get the assignment. I felt that I did a pretty good job, and I learned a great deal. Nonetheless, producers feel that I am limited to multiple-camera shows, that I can't do anything other. I know directors who would love to work in the other types of production, but they haven't been able to get a shot at it.

• *JR:* How about melodrama?

• *NP:* I think I'd be a terrific director for noncomedic stuff. I don't particularly want to do thrillers, or Hitchcock-like drama. However, at this time, only *I* know all this. And I may or may not get a chance at anything else. It's a lot of fun to do comedy. Last season I did fourteen *Barney Miller* episodes. By the end of the season I was burned out about it and everybody in it. This year I am doing only ten—probably about the optimum number for a director.

Gene Reynolds

Reynolds is the prototype of the producer-director, the man who desires as much control over his product as is possible in commercial television.

Beginning as a child actor, Reynolds has progressed through writing, direction, and production. Some of the most unusual television series of the past two decades have been directed or produced by Reynolds.

Television series: Wanted, Dead or Alive; 77 Sunset Strip; Room 222; Peter Gunn; NYPD; My Three Sons; The Munsters; Mannix; Hogan's Heroes; The Ghost and Mrs. Muir; F-Troop; Anna and the King; The Donna Reed Show; M*A*S*H; *and* Lou Grant.

- *John Ravage:* Some other directors were considering the remarks you made about the videotape experiment that you're going to have with *M*A*S*H*. They thought that you would be unsuccessful, or the experiment probably wouldn't work to your satisfaction.
- *Gene Reynolds:* It might not. The point is that at least we will satisfy ourselves.
- *JR:* Is film really as dead as everybody has said it is?
- *GR:* On, no. I don't think that; I hope not. It would be a shame. We've lost the one-hour tape drama on t.v.—e.g., *Philco, Studio One.* They should have one show like that on t.v. today. It would provide some actors, directors, writers—we should not lose the one-camera comedy.
- *JR:* There is esthetic reason for not using tape, also.
- *GR:* Well, that's what they're talking about.
- *JR:* Whether we like it or not, this is what it's going to be?
- *GR:* Well, esthetics give way to the economics.
- *JR:* Every time?
- *GR:* Well, practically every time. That's what part of the audience felt was going to happen by turning to tape. They're going to go to tape on *Police Story.* Maybe they're going to

compromise the quality. I don't know. I just talked to the cameraman this morning. He shares my position. He says that he'd like to try it, to see how it works. It's a matter just of not closing our eyes to change. It's not only economics, it has to do with a whole business built on a sophisticated, electronic, high-speed technology.

• *JR:* How are you going to fight that?

• *GR:* It's coming. It's like the guy who says he's sticking to the horse: "I don't care about those damn motors you got there, I'm sticking to the horse because the horse knows me when I call it." There's a certain kind of inevitability, I'm afraid, about this whole electronic approach to t.v.

Last Thursday night, Ron Beckman came down and said, "If you want to, we can try your last show on tape, one-camera tape." I was curious. I talked with the cameraman, and he feels that if we light it properly and the guys don't fool around with the fine tuning too much, then we can get quality comparable to one-camera film. I don't know how much we'd gain, because you've still got one camera.

• *JR:* Who do you think of as good television directors?

• *GR:* Well, in my field, I think Jay Sandrich is good; Hal Cooper is good, and Hy Averback. Jackie Cooper is good. Those are the guys I know the best.

• *JR:* What makes them the best?

• *GR:* First of all, there's mechanics; they can solve mechanical problems well. Then being able to work with the actors to get comedy performances. Jackie Cooper, for instance, uses the single camera well, and he knows where the laughs are; he knows how to get good performances out of people. The same with Hy Averback and Jay Sandrich—they know their business; they're not losing laughs. Many directors of comedy are not truly comedy directors because somehow a certain humor is lacking. I sometimes find what I consider to be the funniest stuff—and the director has the actor walk upstage. Not that we should have to cut to a big close-up on every joke, but some really important humor is lost. It shows a lack of sensitivity to what the writers want.

• *JR:* Do you think the best directors come out of an acting background?

• *GR:* No, some directors who miss the laughs are actors too, or ex-actors.

Hy Averback stages very well. He lays out his work well. In other words, his coverage is intelligent. If there is a character in the show who is an outside character, Hy handles him well. If it's a general, he doesn't let him get too big or too small, that kind of element: having a certain amount of taste.

• *JR:* Many of the actors on *M*A*S*H* mentioned that they don't like the direction of Jackie Cooper. Yet you rate him at the top. I wonder how there could be such polarized views. In other words, could you be using a different yardstick to judge what a good director is than do the actors?

• *GR:* Some actors respond to different directors. I think that it's just possible that there might have been personality problems in this case. He does get out of the script what the writers intended . . . and more. An actor may not like working with a director and yet he does his best work with him. Quite often we are the worst judges of what we do. Jackie is a very powerful personality and it's possible that some actors don't like that in a director.

• *JR:* Harry Morgan was telling me that he thinks the best directors are ones who have been actors. He remarked about Jackie in particular that he enjoyed him; he thought he was good at what he did.

• *GR:* You can't generalize though. A director who is a former actor can be very aggressive and then he can have kid gloves, be gentle and easy.

• *JR:* Jay Sandrich, for instance, does not have an acting background, yet he is considered to be among the best.

• *GR:* I was surprised the other day when he said that it's easier for a director to work with one camera than with three cameras, because he gets a lot of help. God knows you get a lot of help in a three-camera situation, when the crew and cast are together all week—the input of the actors, the camera director, whoever is helping to line up the cameras. You've got a master if you can stage brilliantly. There's no question that you can direct very well under these circumstances. There aren't nearly the alternatives that you'll get with one camera. With one camera you do a sequence, and the number of shot choices is infinite. I don't think the number of choices with three-camera shows is infinite. Once it's staged it's a matter of shooting the master and a couple of cuts, whether they are close-ups or over the shoulders and little else. With one camera you can make an infinite number of choices. You can set on a close-up; you can set on the horses' hooves; you can set on a long-shot, you can set on zooming; you can do any number of things.

• *JR:* But when you're working in real time, in front of an audience, doing a play, everybody has repeatedly said that you're limited by time and the ability to move the equipment.

• *GR:* I think the experience in the booth with tape is more difficult.

• *JR:* M*A*S*H has, since its moment of inception as a series, dealt with serious material in a comedic vein. What do you think about the director's control over the content of the program?

• *GR:* The director is, primarily, an interpretative artist. He's not a creative necessity as is the writer. Content, basically, finds its genesis in the writer, not the director, in television.

In features it's different. In feature films the director is often the writer of the screenplay—in which case he is the writer. If he has not written the screenplay, he has worked on the material to such a great extent that he makes a great creative contribution. Some directors are *auteurs* and some are not. At any rate, I am not crazy about the *auteur* theory. I believe in the collaboration between writer and director, and I think this whole *auteur* thing has been a phase. In television, the director is interpretative, for the most part. He is handed the script. He must objectively understand what the writer is about and what the story is about. He must understand the characters, what their goals are, and what the whole thing adds up to—and find the best way to interpret all that.

• *JR:* Have you ever refused a script—said it's not good, that you wouldn't do it?

• *GR:* I've turned down scripts because I thought they were rotten, sure.

• *JR:* I mean one whose outline you may have eventually used, but said as a director, "I won't direct this. This idea is no good."

• *GR:* One of the problems of free-lance directors is that they don't have much opportunity to accept and reject. Some of them do. But if you're just gypsying around, you're likely to anger somebody, so you're very apt to take something and just do it. You can respond to the script and argue that its intention is not fulfilled. The director should be very keenly aware of what the hell the writer is saying: if it's convoluted or confused or not clear, if it's too obvious or whatever—there should be a definite interplay between writer and director, producer and director. I really believe in collaboration in writing and direction. I believe in the writer being on the set, being helpful during rehearsal and during shooting. And I think that this sizzling dichotomy between writer and director in this town is ridiculous; it's terrible.

• *JR:* I have talked to writers about these issues and been told two things: If you ask them to come on the set, they're too busy, they're off; they're doing treatments for five other shows. They wouldn't come anyway. Then I've talked to writers—in one case, exactly the writer who was being referred to by a producer as unwilling to show up. He said, "I'd love it. I'd show up every day. I wouldn't ask for any more money. I would like to be there." How do you view this problem?

• *GR:* That varies. I think both examples are true. They really are. I have writers whom I have invited to a reading because I thought I was doing them a favor. They have come to the reading and said, "I hate to get up so early in the morning. Do we have to come to these things?" I say no. They don't seem to want to come. They believe that they've done their job, and they're content to stay home and write. It's especially true of many television writers. If they came to all the shootings of their work, they'd be half as productive as they are. Because they would sit around for eleven or twelve hours a day just watching the actors.

• *JR:* Are the stages always open to every writer so that he may attend if he wants to, or is it only with some directors?

• *GR:* A friend of mine wrote *Sybil.* A director threw him off the set. The director was insecure; he forbade his being on the set. Then the director was fired, and the next director was fired, and the next director was delighted to have him. So the writer is not always secure; the writer does not always know that he's welcome.

• *JR:* Do you think that it would be helpful for writers to know that they could come and watch their product be put into shape?

• *GR:* It would be great. The only problem is that there are some very up-tight directors who don't want the writer around. Also, there are certain writers who can be a terrible pain in the ass, who object to line readings.

That's principally what this sizzle developed around—somebody felt that it was going to be costly, take too much time. First of all, the egos involved militated against this kind of collaboration. Then the production office said, "Don't let the writer come on the set; he won't be content with what the director's decided to do." Myself, I think that that kind of collaboration is possible. Admittedly, it's a problem if the writer is there; there is no longer one "master" on the set, and the actors often are sensitive to this. Even without being conscious of it they turn to the writer and say, "Can you help me with this line?" instead of digging out a motivation by themselves. They'll start looking for help, and this detracts from the authority of the director. So there are problems.

It wouldn't bother me. I would love to have them; however, I think the director must have the last word. If there is a problem, if the director is losing control because the actors are running to the writer or the writer is being too difficult, then the writer has to go. He cannot divide the authority.

• *JR:* Do you have any opinions about what the government's position ought to be concerning television content?

• *GR:* Well, I was very much opposed to the "family hour." I thought it was a step toward a greater violation of the First Amendment. I don't think the FCC should have told the networks to do something about content. I think that the whole thing should be worked out between the artists and the networks. There are content problems about sex and violence. There must be responsibility in broadcasting.

I don't look at television in the same way as motion pictures. In television there is immediate access to people's minds through the tube, and there must be a sense of responsibility by producers and broadcasters. There was tremendous hypocrisy in the family hour and I thought that it was an encroachment by the government on artistic freedom, and I was very much opposed to it. The people who are objecting to the family hour seem to be contradicting themselves, and I seem to contradict myself when I say there must be greater responsibility in broadcasting; it seems like a contradiction. How you achieve this kind of taste and discretion is the issue. It was achieved incorrectly.

• *JR:* It doesn't take very long to realize this is the cheap-shot way of using the media. It makes jobs and fills screen time. *Starsky and Hutch* is an example of this. Does that violate your sensitivities or not?

• *GR:* Yes. *Starsky and Hutch?* Of course. Advocated by the very networks that are imposing the family hour; that's why I say it's hypocritical. There are so many shows on that use gratuitous violence. I see shows where the heroes grab a guy, and they try to get some information out of him, so they bend him over and throw him head first into an iron fence, and he starts to holler. Then they don't just let it go at that; they throw him against the fence again. I've seen this in a show six times, six times! Not only was it horrifying, but it was boring, this terrible repetition. Finally the guy is so beaten up that he begins to talk. That's awful, awful. But it's the network that approves of that and accepts that which at the same time, turns around and says, "You know from 8 to 9 you can't say 'hell' or 'damn.' " Terrible hypocrisy.

• *JR:* If a director or producer says that he won't do the material because of its lack of responsibility, what happens to him? Let's say it's, for example, *Starsky and Hutch,* and it calls for exactly that scene you just described, and the director says, "I will not do that." He would probably get fired, right?

• *GR:* You mean if a certain amount of violence is called for and he doesn't turn it in?

• *JR:* Yes.

• *GR:* Now you're getting back to the Nuremburg trials. There's no question that the directors could refuse to do violent shows, and some of them do. Unfortunately, I don't think that's the answer. If a director is an "action" specialist, or if he does dramas and is a good action director and he works for Quinn Martin, or Universal, I'm sure that he can go in and tell the producer that instead of actually seeing the guy get hit in the mouth, "we shoot it in such a way that the action is obscured and you won't really see it." If they then say to him that they want to see the hit in the mouth . . . well, if he doesn't do it they won't hire him anymore. It's possible, I would say. I would say if he tried to take all the violence out of those shows the producers would be alarmed.

• *JR:* So the director really has no defense?

• *GR:* Free-lance directors do not have a great deal of defense. I think that some directors are responsible and do action more tastefully than others. There have been some who have no taste and love violence; they feel that it's going to put real virility in the show.

There are actors who are extremely eager to project an image of virility. They're dying to grab people and shake them up; it's a great temptation to the actor to act manly, because subconsciously he knows that the character actor or the stunt man is not going to hit him back. All of this macho urge, this violent urge comes out. There are many actors whose level of comment is very primitive. They love to take their shirts off; they love to knock the guy through the plate glasss. To them, that's action.

• *JR:* I'm sure that you're aware of the arguments raised against *M*A*S*H* and its use of sex as a toy, a plaything, a mild diversion. There never seems to be a meaningful relationship.

• *GR:* You've got to *look* at *M*A*S*H* though. We don't emphasize sex that much. We receive all kinds of interpretations of our shows. Look at *M*A*S*H*; look this year and see how many times Hawkeye had any kind of sexual conversation with a nurse. Out of twenty-four scripts in a year there are only one or two that stress sex. It's not exactly like *Starsky and Hutch,* where there's action in every reel. What I'm saying is that we have leaned away from that. Undoubtedly, there was implied in the feature that the doctors were having the nurses, and . . .

• *JR:* Implied rather strongly.

• *GR:* We have leaned away from that. We've had Hot Lips and Frank carry on a relationship, but Hawkeye is not a billy goat. Although you may remember it one way, perceptions vary. I don't think there's anything wrong with his liking girls, and I don't think there's anything wrong with his pursuing girls—it's the girls, his attitudes toward the girls. Does he look at them as just something that will just roll over for him? Do they look at him and say, "Oh, my God, it's Hawkeye," and fall over backwards? Do they not tell him to get lost? Do they not reject him? Do they not stand up to him? Are they not portrayed as people and not as objects?

Very often we look at a show and we don't really see it the way it is. Our perceptions are influenced by something we're projecting.

● *JR:* Perceptions being what they are, there have been remarks in well-known publications that *M*A*S*H* is sensual in the most Old Testament tradition.

● *GR:* It's incorrect. I'm not responsible for incorrect perception. I do not have Hawkeye treating women as did Philip Marlow: the door would open, the girl would look at Philip Marlow from the tip of his toes to his hat and say, "Come in." The whole implication was that a woman took one look at him and said, "I'm yours." That would be a treatment of women as some kind of easy sexual object.

Boris Sagal

Sagal began directing in New York City during the live production days of the 1950s. He directed for Playhouse 90, Hallmark Hall of Fame, *and most of the network "theaters" during that era.*

Most of his work in television has been in the direction of long-form productions.

Television: The Money-Changers; Rich Man, Poor Man; A Case of Rape; *and* The Gary Powers Story.

● *John Ravage:* Is there anything unique about television directing that makes it different from directing for the theater or directing for feature release films?

● *Boris Sagal:* I think there is one element; it's not a profound element, and it isn't any great inventive element. What you have to develop to survive in television is terrific efficiency. Efficiency with time, with creative effort, with all the creative disciplines used in preparing the script, working with the actors, working with the producer, and shooting in the allotted schedule, because of a very fixed budget. So what you develop, if you want to survive, is just plain efficiency.

I am a director from the theater. I have my master's from the

Yale School of Drama. I was always theater-oriented, and I've directed half a dozen feature films. So I've had an opportunity in all of these areas. I would say that television teaches you an economy of choices. It's self-explanatory, isn't it?

• *JR:* Would you, then, consider yourself an "actor's director?"

• *BS:* I think that if you're a director, you're a director. I think I work well with actors because I was an actor myself. That helps. I think one of the crucial problems is working with the actor to help him get a reasonably good performance in the allotted time. He is terribly pressured, because of the time element in television, to come up with something. To put him at ease so that he can operate in a creative fashion, to relax him and to give him guidelines in interpreting a character that he has to make come to life, that is a key job of a director; but that's directing. It is as important as watching the camera and selecting your angles and working with the lighting. A director should be an actor's director but he should be a camera director as well. I've directed for twenty-two years, and I really don't feel that you can make hard and fast rules. Some programs are strictly performance shows. You really have to work on the characterization and the acting. And some shows are just the cop-and-robber show, or a melodrama—it's all action. It's foolish to waste a lot of time on them. The emphasis there has to be on the storytelling element, the plot, to not give away the Hitchcock ending. I can't tell you how they used to worry on that show about giving away the ending. The only time the producer ever showed up was when they shot the last scene. You'd never see him all week until the last scene was scheduled.

Those producers don't have material written by Horton Foote or Paddy Chayefsky—though neither of them now writes for television. There are those who do write with a great emphasis on character, the relationship between people. Both have their values, I guess.

• *JR:* Any particular way in which you prefer to approach actors and the script?

• *BS:* Ideally, if there is time, I would like to spend a day reading the script with the actors around the table, with the writer there, discussing all the dramatic values with them. And if there are any problems—anything that they feel they can't make articulate, anything that they feel is obscure—the writer will get a lot of ideas just hearing people read the script. Scenes that they only heard in their bedrooms or were typing in their office come to life just because people are reading them—and certain lines don't sound good.

Actors, you know, profess themselves, they can tell you right there, "Gee, this doesn't look comfortable," or "I don't think I can handle this," or "I don't know what this means." The time that saves you when you are shooting is tremendous, because you solve a lot of the things, a lot of the hitches that hold you up. Also, if there were time, I'd like to have a writer on the set. I love having a writer around because it's a big load off me if I say, "Joe, we've got to have another line here" or "This scene isn't going." And he can go to a typewriter. You don't have that luxury in television.

• *JR:* Certainly there is a difference between situation comedy and the longer forms. The writers are constantly walking in and out of the rehearsals, for instance.

• *BS:* Well, that is a technique they use in sit-coms and I think it is very effective.

• *JR:* But they're concerned with jokes a lot. *Jokes.*

• *BS:* And the writer is there. Remember, the sit-com is still the old live television process or the old theater process. It's a matter of rehearsing a week and taping the last day. You don't have that in motion pictures. It wouldn't quite work in films because of the short scenes that you need in the storytelling process. You don't have to rehearse it once or twice and then shoot. Sit-coms are basically verbal situations. There is very little character. There are a lot of "types" of people. You recognize them right away. In two lines you know that is the boss.

• *JR:* You don't have to build the character?

• *BS:* No. This is the hen-pecked husband, the domineering wife; this is the harassed housewife; this is the obstreperous teenager.

• *JR:* Everybody is saying that film is dying rapidly in television because of the costs. The major studios are investigating the cost of electronic vans; most have no t.v. facilities.

• *BS:* Well, I don't see anything wrong with that. I don't think it alters anything, basically.

• *JR:* You don't think it will change the long-form and the melodrama?

• *BS:* I would like to do the long-form on tape. I don't see why not. I think it's merely a matter of learning the technique. It's shot pretty much like film. You don't really alter it that much. You have to shoot tape-scripts a little more closely, and you still suffer a little bit from the lack of quality in tape, I think. Overall, I'd say it doesn't make much difference, because on a small screen you can't detect that difference.

But a lot of the long-form shows are released as features in Europe or in the Far East, and very often they have to consider that market; it's important to them. You really can't release a tape show in the theater. You can transfer, but you do lose a lot of quality. But I think it is a matter of time. But I'd go to tape if it's cheaper. I think it's all a matter of economics, not at all that one is better than the other. By and large that dictates everything. You know, in television it's business, unfortunately. In motion pictures you always feel that, well, a little extra investment might earn more in the box office. Because audiences may like the picture better. But you can't feel that way with television. You don't necessarily get any more money back.

- *JR:* At best, if a series is amazingly successful a year from now, you might get it back.

- *BS:* Well, you're talking about series. I haven't done a series in maybe ten years. I've done nothing but long-form television. So I'm not at all familiar with what has happened to television series as such, though it seems to me that they are diminishing in numbers, at the least the filmed ones. People are getting bored with series. Even *Police Story* is almost an anthology.

- *JR:* You mentioned that there is some kind of conceptual difference between television and film.

- *BS:* Listen and beware of rules. They are all generalizations that mean absolutely nothing. I think the material dictates the way you're going to shoot it. I don't think that shooting a feature, a theatrical feature, ought to differ from shooting a television film, except for time. And because of time and money you just have to be more efficient, more clever to make your points. You have a lot more time in features to make mistakes, to change your ideas, to shoot masters from different directions, to change angles. Rules don't work; I don't know who makes those things up. They mean nothing. Sometimes I'll do a show, and I'll shoot a whole scene in a master and walk away from it. Another time I'll come to a scene and do everything just with close-ups or with individual shots. The material dictates.

You know, very often you don't get a chance to see your set until practically the night before you shoot a television show. If you're shooting locations you walk in on a set that's new to you. It might be a room like this, and I have a scene with three people arguing in it. I'm not going to try to hold a master in a room like this. This is just not necessary, particularly if I want to move around to other stages so that the characters can get out, have activities that suggest another life different from what they were talking about. No way. I think the traditional way of shooting movies still applies as a basic rule—with a million exceptions. It's always good to get a master, for two reasons: 1) for emphasis, for dramatic emphasis, and 2) for tempo. You may feel that you can't have the actors play a certain sequence any faster because they have to make transitions from one idea to another. But, if you have enough coverage, you can go from close-up to close-up or a two-shot to a two-shot a little faster than they actually played it. You take the pauses out, and you speed up the scene. You emphasize the scene by using one act or one character more than the others. By using the reactions you may throw the dramatic value in a different direction. But, basically what your master does is to give you and the editor a reference point, a geography. You see the map of the scene. You can say, "Well, let's follow this river," or "We'll go up this like," or "We'll take this road." That's what you're trying to say and every scene should try to say something—if it's a decent scene.

The more film you have the more possibilities you have of what the scene is about. However, at the same time that I say that, there are constant exceptions. But I know that if you're learning how to shoot film or how to direct you must think in terms of a master; it makes life simpler. Stage it in terms of a master, you know, for yourself.

As I got more fluent and learned, I got to the point where I very often let the actors dictate the shot. If you have the time, you walk in and say, "Look, this is the scene. What's it about?" Let us say that a husband and wife are to decide that they're going to get a divorce. They just don't want to sit down and talk because they are uncomfortable about it. So, it's early morning. He's got to go to

work; she's got to go to work. They've got to make breakfast.
They've got to eat and they've also got to discuss this terribly vital
thing. Let's figure out a way of doing it. She'll make coffee. He'll
make the toast. He'll bring the newspaper in.

• *JR:* An improvisational kind of thing?

• *BS:* That's the best kind, but not so improvisational that you
don't use the dialogue. Improvisation wasn't written for actors
who change the writer's lines. If the lines don't work, ask the
writer. I don't go for the type of improvisation that Altman does.
He lets the actors write. Now most actors, I find, are highly
creative as actors but not necessarily good writers. Quite to the
contrary, they are quite illiterate. You know, they're terribly
illiterate. An actor isn't necessarily a writer. They all start coming
up with words that are awful—at least a lot of them seem to be
unnecessary. Who in the hell needs that, you know? That's what
writers are for. You wouldn't dare start changing lines on
Broadway. I don't like that. I call the writer if I have real difficulty
with a scene. You'll do an improvisation where you can recall an
experience in his life that made him cry. You can use that experience in playing this particular scene. That's standard in theater.
That's what every good acting coach teaches.

• *JR:* Yet I have had some well-known directors tell me that
they don't know anything about that stuff. "That stuff" refers to
what I call the Strasburg method.

• *BS:* It's a shame. I really feel sorry for them. They should at
least know it; they don't have to use it, but it is another tool. Tools
to work with. Why turn your back on it? When the zoom lens came
out many guys said, "I wouldn't use that zoom lens. That's for
guys that do commercials." You know, that's ridiculous. If it
screwed up my lighting I'd say, "Listen, I don't know the zoom
lens, so why don't you admit that you don't know it? It's another
tool, so let's learn to use it. What the hell, it can't hurt us, you
know, even if we don't like it." Today, of course, we all use the
zoom lens. Unfortunately, there are guys who don't get off of it.

It's the same thing with the "method." You may not agree with
it, and a lot of what the "method" says all the actors know
innately and all directors know it instinctively, even if they don't
articulate it. There's a lot of validity and truth in it. Very often
when you direct you don't teach, you direct. I think it's a terrific

tool. If an actor says it's the way he works, then I think a director should not want to confuse things. I'm not talking about teaching. I ask for results on a stage, and if an actor has trouble getting them, I'll do everything I can to help him find a way to get them. But I don't talk in terms of acting studio workshop terms on a stage. I can do that, if I have to, in a classroom or a workshop. But I can tell immediately when an actor works from the interior. You can tell by the way he starts working on a scene. And when he does, I know exactly how to approach him, because I also know Strasburg and those guys. I was auditing Actors' Studio when I was in New York. During periods of unemployment it was a terrific place to come to. A lot of people did that to listen and find out what was going on.

But I think anybody who says "I don't know anything about that stuff" is really limiting himself. Directors come from all areas.

There are directors who come from film editing, you know; it doesn't make them less of a director, but their whole approach is strictly in terms of editing the film. They never strengthen themselves in other departments. Other directors may come from writing, and they expect the performance to come as a whole "clop." They don't understand why the lines aren't coming out the way they wrote them. And again, there are some very good directors who were writers. I think Walter Doniger started out as a writer, for instance—a good writer.

There's no one way, you know. Someone says, "How do you become a director?" You wouldn't know how to answer that. You have to know a little bit of everything. I try to use everything I can. The older I get, believe me, the more I learn how little I know. You know a lot less after twenty years than you did in the first year, somehow, except that now you know what you don't know.

You are very confident of the basics, but you should feel confident enough to say that you really don't know. I don't know the answer to everything, and that's the easiest way sometimes. Sometimes you get bollixed up with a shot or a scene and twenty guys will step in to help you. It's when your directorial self-image prevents you from saying anything about it that you make problems for yourself.

• *JR:* Some actors that I have seen look and act as if they quite often need more therapy than they do direction.

- *BS:* We all do sometimes.
- *JR:* Every director has to have some kind of audience in mind. Who is your audience?
- *BS:* Myself. I'm really out to please myself. If I'm happy with it, they have to live with it. You assume that you have certain theatrical instincts, and, I think, certain unconscious conventions that you abide by—just as in politics you can be a Democrat or a Republican, but you both agree that the Constitution is okay. Nobody says, "Let's tear it up and start again."

There are certain conventions that you know you have to fulfill from an audience's point of view. If you have a love story, the bad guy isn't going to get the girl, and the good guy is—the audience expects it. That's where you're going to end up. But as for the dramatic development, you really have to please yourself. *You* are the audience for those actors. Tape or film, there's nobody else listening to what they're doing except you.

- *JR:* In television, you're not worried about the producers?
- *BS:* Well, with some you are. I always feel the producer will love everything that I do or he wouldn't have hired me. We're not antagonists. We're together to do it together.

Every once in a while there is an antagonist, and it's unfortunate. It doesn't make for better pictures. We're there to work together and I figure the guy hired me, he's got to love me and I will learn to love him.

- *JR:* You mentioned earlier about having the writer around the set.
- *BS:* I think the real problem is money. A writer has only so many hours, particularly in television; they try to go from show to show. If they were paid enough so that they could write the script and *also* stay for the shooting, they'd be available. Otherwise the guy has time to do it only when he's free. And you can't ask them to give up time; it's money. He works just like any factory man. You just shouldn't invite them; you should make a deal where they are paid for their time. For example, if the writer is not the producer you should pay enough so that he or she is available all during the shooting. That doesn't mean he has to stay there all the time. It would bore him and it would bore you. After a while the very fact that he is there is going to make him feel that he has to

find something to do. You want him to be available, and when you come to a difficult moment you may say, "Hey, Joe, come on in. I want you to watch this scene. It isn't going to work. Something is wrong with it. Come on in and tell me. I'm going crazy and the actors are going crazy." Or he may come in and say, "Let me see what you are doing today." I would say, "Great, hang around. We're going to do this scene or that scene."

The economics are such that producers can't afford to keep a writer that extra amount of time. Now, there may always be some writers, just as there are some directors, who have personalities that make working difficult. Maybe the two of them don't get along, and I suppose the director has to prevail. He has to get on with the show. But that rarely happens. I don't see why that should be a problem unless somebody is an idiot about it.

- *JR:* Does the content of television bother you?

- *BS:* Oh yes, very much. It is a great jungle of mediocrity. There is no question about it. And the best thing you can get out of television is to be successful enough so that you can pick and choose your material—so you don't have to take every job that comes along—because there are also some very fine, intelligent, sensitive things being done in television. There's no question about it. But, with the pressure of production quantity, it's just impossible to produce so many wonderful, pure, creative things. And when you're trying to make a living—a pretty good one—and you're trying to get as many shows as you can, you're going to end up taking a lot of rotten shows that you know are rotten. You're going to try to get through them, but you rely mostly on professional skill and craftsmanship to carry you.

By and large, if you can be in a position that some directors are in, you chosse the material that you want to do as much as possible. You'll sit for a month, maybe two, turning scripts down; at a certain point you've got to eat. There are some guys who live so modestly that they end up doing only one or two shows a year. That's good enough for them. A lot of directors aren't in that position, they just aren't. They're not given choices. I've been working at it long enough, and I'm fortunate that I've had enough successes so I can pick and choose.

- *JR:* Have you ever walked out on a production because of its content?

• *BS:* Yes. I refuse to do shows because of content, oh, I'd say 50 percent of the time at least. I have refused to do shows that I felt were excessively violent and had nothing redeeming about them. And, I might add, I like violence if it's integrated, if it's meaningful. I refuse to do shows that I think are just mindless or idiotic. If I needed the dough, I'd say, "Yes, of course, I'll do it." But whenever I don't need the money that badly, why, you know, it's meaningless. I don't want to die with an anonymous tombstone. I'd like to say I did a few things that meant something. For example, I did *Case of Rape* with Elizabeth Montgomery, a very meaningful show which changed legislation throughout the country. I also directed *The Money-Changers,* which was just out recently. The same thing, you know. It was not profound; this was a popular show, but at least it was intelligent. It wasn't Ingmar Bergman, but it was an intelligent show. It was a good, articulate, clear show. I was quite happy with it. I wish that it had said certain things about banking that we were never given the opportunity to say or the networks didn't want to hear—the corrupt aspects of it—but I can accept that. We're not out to shake the system; we're out to criticize the system.

• *JR:* Who are really good writers?

• *BS:* Robert E. Thompson, who wrote *Case of Rape,* and who recently wrote *The Gary Powers Story.* Stanford Whitmore is a very fine writer; he did part of *The Money-Changers* with me. Dean Riesner, who did *The Money-Changers* and *Rich Man, Poor Man.* Those are three very good writers. James Costigan, who did *Eleanor and Franklin,* is a very fine writer. These are good people. I think they are ranking writers, and I think they write features as well. Chayefsky doesn't write for television anymore, but I imagine even he would find some subject that really turned him on for a television show. I think he's rich enough to not be concerned with what he's going to make.

• *JR:* Who are directors in television whom you particularly admire?

• *BS:* Well, I think there're a lot of good directors, a lot of talent. I've always liked Fielder Cook, a good director; Alex Siegel, a fine director, a little temperamental and tough to work with, but a very good director.

Most of those I mentioned had a lot of background, not only

university training, but they also came from the theater, and I really think that is—particularly in television—a vital ingredient. They were all stage directors to begin with; that makes a big difference. I had to learn how to work with scripts, staging actors, and directing actors . . . performances.

• *JR:* It seems to me that the bulk of the directors who are working as series directors are more and more being produced by the guild. Kind of so many hours as an aid and then a job.

• *BS:* No, not at all. Not in film television.

• *JR:* Not in film?

• *BS:* No, no. In tape that might be, that might be. But that was always the case in live tape. I was an associate director for a while and a stage manager before I became a director. But I had already been a director for years in the theater. Somehow that seemed to be a natural progression. In film, anybody is a director; you get a job as a director. The majority of our members are one-shot directors. They've done one thing and they enter the guild. They pay a $4,000 initiation fee and are never heard from again, and that's over 50 percent of our membership.

• *JR:* Do you have any views of contemporary television? Content? Directing? Material? Acting? Its direction?

• *BS:* I think the novel form of television is good; I hope it stays a long time. It's much more interesting and I think it's going to be more sophisticated. *The Money-Changers; Rich Man, Poor Man,* that type of thing. I also think the role of the director as a creator should hopefully get a little bit more recognition in television, as it has in feature film. He is a vital element. Very often too many directors pass on a lot of their creative functions to the producer, and it's tragic. They shouldn't do that because they are, in effect, forfeiting some of the functions of a director. In post-production, for instance, they should edit their film. They should stay no matter what the cost. The guild has set up the rules in such a way that you have every legal right to stay with that film as long as you want to and finish it. Too often they abdicate those rights and pass them on to a producer or an associate producer.

• *JR:* Are you saying that they should demand the right to a final cut?

• *BS:* Final cut? Absolutely. A final cut. They should be there up through and including the addition of music. Now the argument is that producers usually don't pay enough. Well, I think they'll pay more when they see how fine your work is going to be. If they don't pay enough? Well, at the next negotiation, try to get more money. But that doesn't mean you should do less work.

The writer should be called in more and more to work in the scripts. It will help the producers. They are called in much too late, and all the producers say it's not very efficient when you're doing ten shows. But not so many are doing ten to twelve series shows. Many are preparing just one. The problem is money. They don't want to pay. Well, that's a mistake. That's money well worth spending. It's up to the director as much as anybody else to become more important in television. The long-form is the hope for television. For the viewer as well as the director. For me to do six and a half hours of *The Money-Changers*, fast and furious, was really an exhilarating experience. I worked with the novel; I worked with the script; I worked with the writers, and I had five months' preparation. It was terrific. I was involved in all the casting. I was involved in all the post-production.

Jack Shea

Currently a member of Norman Lear's TAT Communications' staff of permanent directors, Shea began directing in New York during the 1950s. After serving as a stage manager and assistant director in television, he joined the Air Photography and Charting Service, producing training films for the armed forces in kinescope form. After the service, he joined NBC-TV as an assistant director, taking on the direction of Bob Hope's Awful Truth *special in 1956. For the next ten years Shea produced and directed Bob Hope specials. In the 1960s he produced and directed* Insight *for two years. During the early years of color television, Shea directed specials for Chevrolet. He has been both producer and director on many of his programs and—like most—would prefer to maintain the added control which producing brings.*

Television series: Wonderful World of Disney; Hawaii Five-O; Death Valley Days; Calucci's Department (*pilot*); We'll Get By; The Glen Campbell Show; The Waltons; *and* The Jeffersons.

● *John Ravage:* Do you see anything that makes television directing different from other directing assignments?

● *Jack Shea:* I'm not sure, but let me start with the theater director. A theater director generally has a tremendous amount of time to develop the property. He has time to get rewrites; he has time to make changes; he has time to develop characters, to search for the character with the actors, to work in front of some tryout audiences. And, then, he still fails at times.

The motion picture director has a great deal more time to develop characterizations. He's generally dealing with new characters, so he's interpreting what the writer has written, and he's helping an actor to evolve a character that fits the film. Again, he has time.

The one thing that any television director doesn't have is a lot of time. I'm a believer in preparation. I think that's the key to any operation, whether on stage, in motion pictures, or here. I believe in a working situation that allows you to be loose, to make changes. I don't believe in rigidity which is not open to things which will enhance what you're doing. When doing a situation comedy, whether here at Tandem or any other place here in Los Angeles, they're all done essentially alike. The characters, after the show has been on for a while, are pretty well defined; you can still experiment with them, but there are certain things those characters will do and will not do, so you don't have to search for that. You only have so many days to get the funniest performance that you can, to find out whether the jokes (or lines) in the script work, and to find out whether an audience will enjoy them. We work at a much more streamlined pace, and there is more responsibility on a director because he has to make some of the choices that actors, in other formats, would help you make—or audiences would help you make. You have to say, "Yes, that's going to be funny," and if the audience doesn't laugh, then you've made a mistake. If you have too little laughter, obviously you will not be very well thought of.

In the rehearsal hall, the director is the audience for a cast. If he feels that a script is funny, he tries to instill confidence in the cast so that they will think it's funny. It is very easy in situation comedy to have a cast lose confidence, even in good material. Somebody can make some small negative comment and it can really throw a cast off. They can go out with very good material and not get any laugh, because they have no assurance that they're going to get any kind of laugh. So, one of the things that a good director has to do is to instill confidence in them. In order to do that, I always try to be just as honest as I can. Then my cast knows that if they ask me whether I think a joke is funny or not, I will tell them. Therefore, I don't go around telling everybody, "Oh, that's the funniest thing in the world." They will just not rely on you. They'll end up making their own decisions, and they may be wrong. However, if they believe me, I'll tell them, "Yes, I think it's funny," or "No, I don't think it's funny," or "I think it *might* be funny; I think it's funny if you do it this way."

It's interesting, we were just editing a comedy that is sensitive. It is so easy to make misjudgments: We had a joke in the show we taped last night, an old joke, but it came out of a certain type of character. I listened to that joke for five days, and I knew that there was something wrong with it, and I kept blaming the actor; I thought that the actor was misreading the joke. Suddenly, in the middle of dinner after the first show, we were giving notes to the cast, and it suddenly dawned on me what was wrong with the joke. I had to put in one word, a repeat of the original line. Here at *The Jeffersons* we have the advantage of three producers who are probably the top situation-comedy writers around. We have two executive story editors; we have two story editors, and we have myself and my assistant—all of whom have been around comedy a long time. In dealing with that joke, none of us realized how to make it much stronger. We got no laugh in the afternoon. In the evening, it got a big laugh, just by adding one word. It went by so fast in the afternoon show that by the time the audience realized what had been said, they were on to the next line. Repeating made it a little bit clearer for the audience, and they understood.

One of the things in comedy direction for television in front of an audience is that the director has to do everything he can to simplify the visual, verbal, and movement elements of the script so that nothing gets in the way of a joke. I worked for Bob Hope for many years, and one of the things that he always preached was that you must not do anything that gets in the way of the joke. If you do, the audience is not going to understand it, and they are not going to laugh.

• *JR:* He was a comic, or is a comic, rather than a comedian. I draw a distinction between the two. The people who play "comic drama" are "comedians," acting out a complex comedy situation, whereas a "comic" is a Henny Youngman or a Bob Hope.

• *JS:* You are right. Some of the shooting techniques that I might use on a drama would get in the way of a comedy, whatever kind of comedy it was, because it would distract the eye.

• *JR:* It seems to me that much of the direction of taped television comedy, three-camera, in front of an audience, boils down to simply "matching" shots. There doesn't appear to be very much visual creativity in that kind of approach.

• *JS:* I think what you're saying is absolutely true. If you analyze situation comedy, laughs are very often in the lines. You move the camera from joke to joke, staying with the character. Occasionally you will find a good visual. On a show like *M*A*S*H,* which is a different type of comedy, there is a totally different approach, where there can be possibly more visual creativity. I think the situation comedy that we're doing here at Tandem depends on seeing the attitude of the performer who delivers the line. For instance, all of us here believe in seeing, for the most part, the whole face of an actor; that's why we use a lot of close-up shots. We don't like to have important lines delivered in profile because we don't think they have the same impact as when you can see a person's two eyes. Norman Lear is famous for yelling, "Two eyes. I've got to see two eyes."

• *JR:* We know who the theater audience is. The audience for any given movie is relatively sophisticated; they get out of their homes to go. Who forms your audience?

• *JS:* Well, I think I play to myself and my family to a great extent. The type of comedy we're doing here, like *The Jeffersons,* is not so sophisticated that it wouldn't be understood by reasonably intelligent young people. We really try to be universal in our appeal. I know that certain things in the show appeal to some people more than others. For instance, the "George Jefferson strut"—I used to pride myself on doing the George Jefferson strut in the rehearsal hall to remind him of what it was. Then I found out that the strut was being imitated by kids in grammar school out in our neighborhood. They all used to love to walk like George Jefferson. Therefore, I know that appeals to younger people, grammar school kids; it also appears to appeal to older people.

I don't think of trying to appeal to one person or another in my general directing of a scene. I do think of trying to make a character more appealing. We found that we didn't attract the older teenagers. Although we had some of them, they weren't part of our major audiences. I had an idea to try to make the young couple, Lionel and Jenny, a bit more appealing to older teenagers. So we tried putting music in a couple of the segments, and we had Jenny dancing the way teenagers are doing now; it was loved by the audience. We've had George Jefferson dance, because he's a marvelous dancer. We find that very appealing to teenagers, it's appealing to other people. For instance, Mother Jefferson was a feisty old lady, just loved by older people. That wasn't particularly the reason she was put in there—because she's also loved by others—but we know that they identified with her. They would like to look as glamorous as she looked, and have that kind of character. I don't find myself thinking about audiences too much.

● *JR:* You're telling me that characters and situations are constructed to merely please another segment of the audience you haven't got. That sounds like manipulation of the audience. Somehow this doesn't seem to jibe with what we know of Norman Lear's productions. Archie Bunker probably wasn't conceived of as a character who was going to appeal to a large number of people.

● *JS:* There's always fear and gambling. I think you make the characters as universally appealing as you can, especially if you're in an early time slot. Now, if you're doing *Masterpiece Theatre* on PBS, that's something else again. You're not looking for the same audience *The Jeffersons* is looking for. At the same time that we are looking for a universal audience, we are doing subjects that we find serious enough to have importance to everybody.

For instance, last year we did a show about suicide. I had doubts about how we could do a half-hour situation comedy about suicide and still be funny. But I thought it was immensely funny, and it also had a tremendous message. What we found out was that the suicide rate among black women is the highest in the country. Now, most blacks did not know that.

We had Louise's uncle come to visit last year, and he had been a butler in a rich person's home in Boston all of his life. Now he was retiring, and George and Lionel referred to him as an "Uncle Tom" because he spoke correctly and politely. Again, I thought it was a tremendously funny show, yet it dealt with one black calling another an "Uncle Tom" simply because he acted properly. A production manager at CBS, whom I have known for a number of years, who's black, came to me after the show and said, "Jack, do you realize what you have done for all of us blacks who wear ties and jackets and work for Whitey?" And I said, "No. Is that really that much of a problem?" He said, "Yep, you'd be amazed at how many parties I go to when—because I work for CBS, because I wear a tie to work, because I wear a jacket or a suit, and because I work for Whitey—I'm called an 'Uncle Tom.' " He said, "You have really cleared the air for an awful lot of us." Now, he was only one of several blacks who told me that. We tried to make the character appeal to as much of the audience as we could, because we thought we were making an important point, an educational point—and we were entertaining. We try to do that with our shows. Sometimes the points are not as strong as others; we try.

We try not to get preachy. We did one program this year on the lie detector tests that are being given as a matter of course by many personnel departments across the country. Research found that many thousands of companies force their employees to take lie detector tests—"personnel investigation"—else they cannot get the job or cannot keep it. We did a story about Lionel Jefferson's refusing to take a lie detector test because he felt it was both an infringement on his personal liberties and that people were trying to dig into his head and categorize him. Again, it was a funny show. I think we made an important point.

• *JR:* Maybe a little bit of preaching works, occasionally?

• *JS:* Well, I think it depends on how you do the preaching. As I said, I think what we're trying to do is to get the point across, but still keep it entertainment—not let it become a sermon. That's really what makes it fun; the shows that we all dig into, more than any others, are the ones that have meat to them.

Every once in a while, of course, we just do a flub show, just crazy fun—and that's fine, too. We do try to keep the pace changing so that the shows don't become repetitious. It is difficult in a situation comedy, because I know one network executive once defined successful situation comedy as being in a single room to which everything comes. People ring the door-bell; people slide down the chimney; people run down the stairs; people come in from the kitchen. Everybody comes to that place to do whatever they have to do to the people who live there. You'll find that on the more successful shows; that's essentially the way it's done. For instance: outside sets—we use them occasionally—and every one of the situation comedies uses them occasionally, but the tighter your writing is, the less you have to go outside of the room. Another reason why we don't use more outside sets is because we really like to do a half-hour show in a half-hour for the studio audience. We think that the studio audience understands the story better, responds better, and enjoys it more; it responds by helping the actors give a better performance.

I've had several people who write for other situation comedies write for us. For instance, one girl who had done quite a bit of magazine writing said she would like to try writing a *Jeffersons*. She wrote a far-fetched story that had George getting on a train on the way to Miami; he ran into Jackie Gleason, and then somebody else. I knew this girl was not a dummy, and I said, "How do you get all of that to happen? First of all, you have to get a train; realistically, you have to make a set that looks real; you have to make it look like it's in movement; you have to play all the scenes in here—and who can get the money to pay Jackie Gleason as a guest star?" She said that she had never thought of that.

I find that very often new writers, especially, write without any kind of self-imposed discipline about locales.

● *JR:* Is your background that of a writer, actor, or director?

● *JS:* When I was in college, I first wanted to be a lawyer, but that's like being an actor. Then I wanted to *be* an actor, and by the time I graduated from college I decided that I was much more interested in directing. Then my aim was to be a director, and I achieved that by becoming a stage manager, an associate director, and finally a director. I've also produced some things at the same time I was directing. I produced the *Glen Campbell Show* for three and a half years. I moved around and worked on different types of shows because in this business, directors, like actors and writers, get typed immediately. When I came off the *Campbell Show* people said I was a comedy-variety director. Then I started doing *Sanford and Son,* and *The Waltons,* and they said, "Oh, he does situation comedies and dramas." Now for the last two years I've been doing mostly *The Jeffersons.*

• *JR:* You were lucky to get producers who would let you break that comedy/variety mold.

• *JS:* It's very tough, so now I try to move around just enough to keep my hand in different things. I also find it refreshing to go from here to an hour film drama, single-camera—a totally different concept of staging and shooting, and I love it.

• *JR:* I notice that most directors, be it in one-camera film, three-camera film, or three-camera t.v. shows, rewrite as they go. I've seen them strike out dialogue, add dialogue, and otherwise do the job of a writer. Do you think this is a reasonable employment of a director's skills, that he should have this much control over the content?

• *JS:* I think it's a matter of degree. I certainly think that part of a director's job is doing some rewrites in order to make things work. I think it's an abuse of a director's job if he rewrites to the point of changing the concept of a play. I, too, have seen directors do that, and I disagree. I think it's wrong. I've a couple of friends who do that, and I don't agree. In the twenty years that I've been directing network programs, I have never directed a script in which I did not have to make some changes. Sometimes they were very minor.

In fact, right now the Writers' Guild is asking—as they have in the last couple of contracts—for a "no changes" clause. Well, I think that's totally impossible. They're not only asking for no word changes, but they're asking for no changes in stage direction. After all, that's what I'm there to do. I'm there for more than just staging; I'm there for developing character, for finding the right way to make a joke work.

We had a joke in last night's show in which the character Tom Willis is talking about one of his authors. He says, "One of our authors was talking to me about this only last week." The way it was originally written, he talks about MIZT, the Marital Infringement Zone Theory, to which Helen says, "I call it BULL"—joke. It was originally written with the MIZT reference coming first, then the explanation the "Marital Infringement Zone Theory." I rewrote it by switching the words, and it became a much better joke. It had gone through approximately nine writers, and nobody had seen fit to change it. That doesn't mean that they wouldn't have after a while, but it was easy for me to *hear* comedy. When I'm working with the actors on the stage and I hear them say the lines, I know that the rhythm is wrong. Directors do this all the time.

I will not make major changes without consulting the producers, because I think I would be violating what they expect from me. That happens to be my personal feeling.

I also have a tremendous respect for the word. I find that some actors—very few, but some actors—start by making changes. Before they've read the damn thing, they're saying, "Oh, I can't say that. I should say such and such and so and so." They rewrite virtually every line; it's terrible.

I feel that our best scripts come from outside writers who write and then are given notes and directed to rewrite. It then goes to one of our sets of story editors, who rewrite it again and give it to the producers, who possibly send it back to the other set of story editors to rewrite again. At some point about halfway through this process, I will read a version and make comments. Those will be incorporated into the next version. So, a tremendous amount of work has gone into producing one script before we sit down with the writers, the actors, and read it. Therefore for somebody, on the first reading, to just want to change every line, create a new script, is pretty outrageous. Not that at some later point we can't say, "Gee, I think it's better to do this," or "It might make more sense for me to do this," or "Help me to make this cross if I do this."

• *JR:* One last, general question. What do you think can be done by directors to increase the variety of material that appears on commercial television? It seems that we're going to have sit-coms from 6:30 to 9 o'clock and then we're going to have *Starsky & Hutch* for an hour. It's almost the same thing every night. Do you think that's just the preordained destiny of commercial television?

• *JS:* I think commercial television will give people what they want to see. As long a commercial television is in its present form, I think that's what it's going to be because let's say you do a program which appeals only to a small segment of the population. You put it on a network and get 9 million viewers. That's not considered enough, yet 9 million is a tremendous number of people.

I think what has to happen is that we must get more cable television and more diversification of stations. It may become profitable to have 9 million viewers and still do a show. Many of us felt for a long time that pay cable t.v. would help a lot of this. If you were to pay 50¢ to watch a show and 10 million people also paid 50¢—that's $5 million, which would be plenty to pay for a show and let everybody make big profits. You wouldn't resent paying 50¢ if it was a show that you really wanted to see. I don't think most people would, not with the price of movies today. That kind of a concept could change television, because people would program to smaller groups. It sounds silly for a group of adults to come into the office and rush to see the ratings list: "Did we come out in the top ten? Did we come in eighteenth? Oh, darn, we're down to twenty-seventh this week. Where did we come out?"

• *JR:* I was wandering around, talking to some other people about what effect striving for ratings has upon the cast. In one sense it's quite evident. It produces great physical tension. The only tool an actor has to overcome such a thing is to try to work harder. Obviously that doesn't necessarily work.

• *JS:* I have been in the position of directing shows when I knew the rating numbers were going down. You don't want to come to work; you don't want to face each other.

An interesting thing happened to me the very first year that *The Waltons* was on. I was one of the four or five directors who were directing. It's shot like a motion picture, so you shoot for six and a half or seven days. First you prepare for seven days, then you shoot for seven days. I directed the eighth show the first year; that was the first time I had worked with the company, but the show had not been on the air yet. In September, when the new season was starting, one of the CBS heads had just made a statement in the press to the effect that "Isn't it a shame that the Waltons isn't gonna make it—because it's such a quality show." He was quoted a saying this in the trades, and everybody in the cast was saying, "Oh, God, it's all over." Everybody else, the production staff, and the producers and the directors, believed in it. We loved the material and the characters. That year, the ratings started out low. People began to say that we could make it. I said that if CBS stayed behind us we could make it. CBS did stay behind us. The show started off and it was way down low. Slowly, it started to creep up at a very slight, continuing rate. By January and February, we were still shooting and right up there. Suddenly we were winning.

It was very interesting to watch the cast as the year progressed, because these downtrodden people would do anything to make it right, take any suggestion. It really was funny to see it happen like that.

5

Summary; The Future; Alternatives

The Problems Facing Television

To the directors interviewed it is apparent that the major restriction which commercial television directing places upon its practitioners is that of limited creativity. "You can't say anything of your own," as Joan Darling says. The demands are well known and understood: cooperate with the front office and get the job done on time and under budget—that's all. No producer wishes to have an experimenter as his director; the system will not tolerate variation of any significant sort.

In summary, the major shortcomings of television can be stated relatively briefly:

The volume of the material. "We're consuming ourselves into oblivion," says Fielder Cook. Prime-time commercial television devours approximately 7,560 hours of material per year. Conservatively, this is the equivalent of three hundred or more two-and-a-half-hour dramas—ten times the entire output of William Shakespeare. Odious as this comparison might seem to some, it is a staggering number of productions to bring to life. Yet, every year, this much material is budgeted, cast, and produced on American television. It is little wonder that critics and directors alike cry out for good scripts, writers, and actors. In the present system, things are unlikely to change.

The ratings. No power can dissuade networks from their unending allegiance to the Nielsen ratings and their imitators. Quality and importance of script are inconsequential when weighed against popularity.

Characters cannot grow. The major challenge which any

playwright places before himself or herself is that of character development. No study of the human condition is legitimate if it does not allow for growth and new ideas. In series television this cannot take place; the concept of an implacable, unerring protagonist contributes to repetitious, enervating, dull plot development.

The narrative compulsion. Storytelling is the essence of television scripts. Even if the material is poor and the acting is weak, one would hope that the story line would be clear and interesting. Unfortunately, the narrative structure is overworked—to the exclusion of non-narrative (rhythmic, thematic) formats. Audiences and directors are suffocated with repetitious plots when interesting and enlightening character studies could be done in other—experimental—ways. An interest in unusual programming is not the predominating sensitivity of advertising-oriented networks.

The level. Commercial television caters to the lowest common denominator in the bulk of its offerings. Ironically, this banal fare is produced and directed by some of the most erudite and educated men and women in theater. The compulsion to be successful overrides all other considerations with the majority of production personnel.

The methods. Pat Shields recalled a sequence from the film *The Hucksters* in which Sydney Greenstreet spat on a table at the board of directors meeting of a major advertising firm. As he did so, he said, "Gentlemen, you have just witnessed a disgusting act . . . but you won't forget it." The inference is clear: what is being serviced on television? Ideas? Experimentation? Social concern? No. Most television will stoop to almost anything to attract attention and offers little for us to think about.

If the content of television is to be changed, from where are the best writers, producers, and directors to come? There is no quick and easy answer to this most vital question. If the "best" are lucky, the public will profit.

Hope for the Future?

If any significant change is to take place in television, it must come from ideas generated by members of the profession like those directors interviewed. Few others have the impact which these men and women can bring to bear upon producers and networks. Though they generally feel powerless to effect immediate change, they envision different alternatives for commercial television in the future.

Some, like Jack Shea, foresee teleplays in the serio-comic mold of *All in the Family*, in which popularity and educational purpose can be welded. The unfortunate truth is that once the initial impact of these kinds of drama has worn off, the plots seem to degenerate into studies of inconsequential human activities punctuated by notes of social concern. The Greeks and the Romans mastered this form of comedy, and they found only a limited number of ideas to treat in this fashion.

Ivan Dixon, the pragmatist, finds that he is better off not to consider what might be; television is not part of an artist's serious work. To find artistic fulfillment he must work in independent features or the theater. Television simply cannot support either writers or directors who wish to study, expand, and express ideas. Therefore, commercial television is merely a way of paying the bills; it will seldom be anything else.

Buzz Kulik sees little in the future of television which is not now apparent. "Formulization," stock plotting, and stunted characterizations seem destined to fill the bulk of television time, simply because audiences are addicted to these stereotypes. Only by breaking into new forms can the substance of programming be changed. As long-forms come to emulate the series against which they were devised to compete, the truth of his observation becomes apparent. The formulization of which Kulik speaks tends to underline the importance of meeting audience expectations, not exceeding them.

Any hope for future change in commercial television must be rooted in new ideas and technologies which are only beginning to develop. Potentially the most important of these possibilities is that of programming for specialized audiences. By means of cable systems, satellite relays, microwave interconnections or other—as yet experimental—techniques, it may become possible to program to highly specific audiences which are widely scattered across the country. Only when it becomes possible for an audience to choose from a large number of programs—supported by funds from viewers, advertisers, or the government—will the last obstacle to the qualitative improvement of television be overcome. It is not reasonable to expect that this will happen soon.

The Public Broadcasting Service

This book has dealt with commercial television almost exclusively. Since there is at present only a relatively small national audience for noncommercial programming, and since few directors find their major employment in that industry, the people inteviewed have had little to say about PBS. It should be apparent, however, that primary among the viable alternatives to commercial television is public broadcasting.

Even though the audience for public television is small and limited, primarily, to major metropolitan areas, PBS content indicates what may happen to larger-scale programming if funds can be found to operate the system.

Relegated to tiny budgets, inadequate facilities, and frequent placement on the Ultra High Frequency broadcast spectrum, public television still commands the interest—if not the careers—of most commercial directors. They find in it a place to escape the pressures of the networks as well as a source of new and classic plays which the commercial networks will not underwrite. As Fielder Cook asks, "Who would turn down a chance at Ibsen or Shaw if he got it?" Those who work in public television proudly point to its ability to present specialized programming for small audiences.

On the other hand, not all directors or critics see PBS as a viable alternative to the commercial networks. It tries, so the argument goes, to justify itself by the same yardstick as does any money-making broadcaster: popularity and high ratings. Once it has given in to these demands, it can only seek the methods which will yield larger audiences, which defeats the purpose of specialized programming.

Other directors point out that PBS suffers from censorship and restraints similar to those found in commercial broadcasting. The federal government and member stations work covertly to control program content. In addition, the search for funding from major corporations further compromises a truly public system. As a consequence, **PBS** stations are almost as concerned with offending audiences as are **ABC**, **NBC**, and **CBS**. The offense may be translated into angry letters to Congress or to politicians— which can directly affect PBS' programming.

The growth of a healthy public system is linked to the development of other forms of television: a fourth network (or more), syndicated series production for independent stations, the growth of cable television, and a proliferation of forms of public broadcasting.

The future of television in the United States is as inextricably tied to the present state of programming on commercial networks as it is to the lack of inventiveness and experiment in all video formats. Electronic television will supplant all but the most prestigious programming for both commercial and public television. New ideas and formats are unlikely to develop until novel means of financing television production can be devised. In all, it will be another decade or two before any major changes in content evolve.

6
Parting Shots

Ethics: The Forgotten Dream?

Overwhelmingly, directors see television as a barren place for talent and creativity. In former FCC Chairman Newton Minow's words, it is "a cultural wasteland." If this is so, how can men and women of no small sensitivities remain at work in such an atmosphere? Isn't their continuation as active participants a strong statement about individual lack of responsibility? Yes . . . and no.

There are approximately 1,800 members of the Directors' Guild of America; they include men and women who have directed only one television program or film as well as those who have directed dozens. One estimate has it that only three hundred members can work in any given year—considering the jobs available when all studios are in full production. The chances of employment are small. This high-stakes atmosphere has a double effect upon would-be directors: they are discouraged by the fact that employment is rare and difficult to find, yet they are lured by the chance that, if successful, they will have beaten the odds and be on their way to success and prosperity.

The compulsion to perform is a vital part of all theatrical forms, as any nascent actor will attest. Once having been exposed to the freedom, rewards, and adulation of creative performance, many will do everything in their command to continue. Ethics and, often, common sense do not enter into this decision-making process. Directors simply feel that they must stay in the business.

Even though most directors feel that the content of the scripts with which they must usually work is less significant and less creative than it might be, each seems to believe that he or she can make something worthwhile (or, at least, avoid what is repugnant) by working within the production process rather than abandoning it. Compromise is a highly esteemed quality in a television director. As Walter Doniger states, "Compromise first. Only then you may have to leave." In order to survive, the director must temper his sensitivities with the realities of the process.

Other directors find that the content of most series television is so innocuous that the decision to quit doesn't come up. Similarly, many argue that the business basis of the medium, coupled with its purposeful lack of inventiveness and minimal emphasis on thought-provoking content, preclude any serious consideration of ethics or morality—the medium simply doesn't function in that context.

Few directors have walked out on a production when their personal senses of ethics or decency were affronted by the producer or the material—and with good reason. Most would have kissed their careers goodbye if they had done so. The few who did walk out did so because they could no longer tolerate a producer, actor, or script; the experience was a pivotal point in their careers. Of those who were interviewed—admittedly an unscientific sample—the ones who walked out found that their prestige was enhanced after the incident. Needless to say, those who were not so fortunate are no longer available to comment as directors.

The commercial television process is no place for those who consider ideas to be more important than popularity. The system rewards those who can tap the common interests of a large segment of the viewing public with vapid nostalgia, sentimental romance, unctuous father figures, wisecracking detectives, or precious family groups.

During the early years of network television, programs included a relatively full range of drama: comedy, fantasy, melodrama, and social drama. Those formats have disappeared in favor of repetitious melodrama and family-centered comedies. Directors decry the lack of dramatic variety as much as do television's harshest critics. Having little choice but to continue in the medium, directors nevertheless wish to get out of television in favor of the greater expressive freedom of the film. Most can only wish; they will never achieve that goal.

Therefore, directors are less concerned with ethics than with pragmatism. Hoping for work in long-form television or motion pictures, all have decided to remain in an imperfect environment on the small chance that some stroke of happy circumstance will enable them to break away from the networks and move into directorial situations which will test their skills and allow them more control over the final product. They have not forgotten their dreams, but reality has tempered their vision. They keep their tools as sharp as possible, hoping.

The Newest Technologies

Television content and form have changed almost continuously over the past three decades. Change, of course, is not synonymous with improvement. Much of the evolution of television can be equated with the development of new technologies.

Those directors who have remained most productive have been the ones who could understand and adapt to changes in engineering. As electronic television comes to dominate production, those directors who have training in this aspect of programming become popular with producers. As newer devices and techniques become available to producers, those who can adapt to them will prosper and find outlets for their creativity.

There are two aspects of change as it applies to such creative endeavors: one deals with the technology itself; the other relates to the content, and the way these changes will affect it.

Within the next two decades, television production will use a variety of new devices to aid in the presentation of ideas. Any listing done in 1978 will rapidly become out of date, but it is obvious that some of these developments will have a large impact upon programming. For instance, experimentation is now being done with holography (the three-dimensional projection of images which can be seen without special glasses or polarized projections), thin-screen, wall-mounted viewing screens which require no "tubes"; improved video-recording and playback units for home and industry; wide-screen images (often projected) which emulate the wide-screen vistas of modern motion-pictures;

and ultrafine-scan television cameras which make possible virtually instant editing and production of *film*.

Additionally, "immediate feedback" systems (enabling the viewer to respond to the content of programs) are already on trial in parts of the United States. The immediate manipulation of content by viewers has enormous implications for future uses of mass communications devices.

Computer-linked television will affect entertainment and education as it brings material into the home which can change society and many of its institutions. Television then may increasingly be joined with the arts to stimulate new experimentation in music, dance, and the plastic and graphic arts.

Obvious, also, is the growth of personal communications devices like Citizens Band (CB) radio and remote telephones. It is not out of the question to imagine the day in which CB-television becomes a part of our mania for projecting our personas to other persons by immediate—and graphic—methods.

As the technology evolves, the potential for expressing ideas will change also. For example, the video-cassette recording device is becoming popular in the United States. With it, viewers can record any material that is broadcast and some which they generate themselves. Though the gadgetry is intriguing, the major impact of this device has yet to be felt. Clearly, a new supply industry will furnish tapes and repairs; others will sell taped versions of special events, motion pictures, and television programs. Ultimately, original programming for this new format will involve production companies which will write and produce new materials. Directors may find—at last—an outlet for more specialized programming which will allow greater creative control than do the networks.

It is probable that television—in one form or another—will become the predominant communication tool of our society. The desire to collect, store, and project images may well become the most pervasive part of our materialistic civilization; a close brush with George Orwell's totalitarian surveillance devices of *1984* is more than a remote possibility.

The most stimulating prospect is that of the program variety which may be engendered by these developments. This may bring about a true revolution in content which would help answer the most severe criticism of directors, writers, and producers alike. A large, diverse audience—one whose needs may be met with new technology—would motivate a full range of dramatic expression akin to the early years of television. Hopefully, this will affect all parts of the entertainment media. If so, we will all benefit—artist, critic, and audience. If not, the status quo may be sustained in new packaging.

Art or Artifice?

The author has studiously avoided the term "art" as it pertains to commerical television. "The word just doesn't belong in this context," says Walter Doniger. His injunction seems well taken, in most respects. Unless it is being loosely used as a synonym for skill, the word seldom occurs in the interviews in this book; most of the directors interviewed don't think of their work in those terms. In short, "art" is not a viable part of commercial television. It is not viewed as such by most producers, directors, writers, or critics.

If a functional definition of art may be said to include a unique view of the human condition as expressed in one medium—or a combination of media—then there is little argument about commercial television's lack of ability to contain such viewpoints. The stress upon popularity and sales potential seems to preclude the originality inherent in any art.

However, if the term can be treated, as it is by those who labor in the business, as a verbal equivalent for skill and training, another set of conclusions may be drawn. Directors take great pride in being able to achieve small victories over those who seem less sensitive. They are eager to manipulate producers and networks in order to carry out a creative piece of editing or an unusual character development. Admittedly, the joys and successes are small.

Some find their greatest joys in relatively minor achievements. Directors of television advertisements may cast aside considerations of the overcommercialization of our society and emphasize, instead, the "style" of creating a story, replete with characterization, atmosphere, and pacing in thirty seconds—much like the makers of early silent movies.

Others pride themselves on their ability to manipulate rehearsal schedules so that there is time to construct long master sequences, allowing characters to build their relationships in a unified, dramatic fashion, as in the theater.

To yet others, finding the time to improvise is regarded as an achievement of note in a medium not readily adaptable to a free and easy discussion of thoughts and motivations between director and actor. Even the long-forms do not easily lend themselves to the use of theatrical techniques intended to clarify or intensify dramatic characterizations. Usually, improvisation gives way to the pressure to get things done as rapidly as possible by depending upon stereotypes.

Artists or not, the directors studied felt that they were the best judges of the qualitative and quantitative content of their programs, even though this critical position is normally denied to them and made the province of the producer.

Denied his creative integrity, the television director has two alternatives: bend to the system or leave. Since the opportunity of working in a truly important art form is nil, most choose to stay in order to learn and be available for that moment when their skills might be called upon to do something worthwhile, of which they will be proud. In that sense, they are constantly alert to new material that might contain an interesting or significant dramatic insight, a script that will allow them to take part in the presentation of some important statement in a form that audiences will understand and find popular.

Glossary

Action sequence. Any dramatic segment featuring movement rather than dialogue; often used as a euphemism for "violence."

Airing. A synonym for "broadcasting." The "air date" is the date of initial network broadcasting.

a.d. or assistant director. The director's aide; a union classification for "journeyman director." He or she carries out the mechanical details of production such as posting rehearsal schedules, coordinating producers' and directors' meetings, and directing secondary actors in sequences.

Auteur. François Truffaut's (and others') conceptualization of the director as "author" of the filmed rendering of another writer's script; one who creates something not evident in a script alone.

Block-booking. An outlawed practice in which films were released only to studio owned and operated theaters, thus assuring a commercial return on any film. It also effectively limited competition.

Blocking. The placing of actors in specific positions for the delivery of their lines or reactions.

The business. Short for show business; a catch-phrase used to refer to all of television, film, and the theater.

Comedy. In commercial television, any "non-dramatic" story line. Comedy and drama are terms which are treated as if there were a continuum with "comedy" at one end and "drama" at the other.

Cover. Synonym for "master." Often used to mean the "protection" of a final edit achieved by purposely shooting more footage than can be used.

Cut. See "edit" (also means "stop" on the sound stage).

Drama or "dramatic television". In commercial television, any "non-comedic" or serious story line (see "comedy").

Dubbing or looping. Adding sound after filming or videotaping is complete.

Edit. To join pieces of film or videotape so as to compose an intelligible sequence, often integrating close-ups into a master. Also used as a noun, an "edit" being a single such combination.

Electronic revolution. The current changeover of many film studios and production companies to videotape technology.

Electronic television. Generic term for videotaping or other, similar, as yet undeveloped, recording techniques (as distinct from "film television").

Episodic television. A generic term for series (serial) programming.

Extras or "dress extras". Actors who have no lines or important characterizations. In t.v. and film, all are members of the Screen Extras Guild.

Family hour. A now-abandoned programming rule in which the first two hours of prime-time viewing each evening were to be free of violence and sexual innuendo.

Feature. Synonyms: movie, theatrical-release film, motion picture, film.

Final cut. The producer's edited version of his program; has to be approved by the network before airing.

First cut. The director's edited version of his program; has to be approved by the producer. Not all directors have a "first cut privilege," but the most influential ones do.

Gypsy. A freelance director.

Hype. Exaggerated claims about content, acting, writing, or direction. Literally, "a shot in the arm" to influence audiences to accept the product before it is shown.

Improvisation. A directorial technique in which actors are encouraged to experiment with dialogue and characterization through spontaneous invention of lines and movement, until a pleasing esthetic product is reached. Improvisation is seldom employed in television because of the press of time and the worries of producers.

Live. Shown on the network as it is being performed, as were all programs prior to kinescope and videotape processes.

Live-taped. Videotaped in front of an audience. The program is acted out like a play, recorded in a theater-like setting, and edited later.

Long-form television. Generally, any television format of ninety minutes' duration or longer. Specifically, "television movies," "specials," and "pilots."

Looping. See "dubbing."

Master. A sequence shot as it happens, in real time, with one camera to catch all action. Later, close-ups are edited into the master for variety and emphasis.

Material. Scripts or ideas.

Melodrama. A dramatic form which stresses plotting, irony, reward of virtue, and poetic justice; commonly the stuff of series television programs.

Moment. A relatively short period of time which may be expanded or contracted to fulfill the needs of characterization. Ordinarily, it is used in series television to lengthen or shorten the running time of the program.

MTM. Mary Tyler Moore Productions.

Multiple-camera technique. A technique in which several cameras simultaneously record a performance. Later, in post-production, the separate films or tapes are edited into a final release version. The multiple-camera technique is essential to electronic television.

Network production office. Usually not an office, as such. Generally, this is the department of a network vice-president whose responsibility it is to oversee a series, noting potentially adverse subject matter, dialogue, or other content.

Network representative. Censor. Each production has its own network official who searches out "offensive" script matters.

Novel for television. A long-form in which the material is based upon a best-selling (or possibly not-so-best-selling) novel.

One-camera. See "single camera."

Outline. A sequence-by-sequence explanation of a writer's idea for a script.

Pages. The basic unit of television production. A program is measured in "pages" which approximate forty-five seconds of running time.

PBS. The Public Broadcasting Service. A television network authorized by Congress and controlled by the Corporation for Public Broadcasting (CPB).

Pilot. A long-form production which has the potential to be made into a series.

Pre-emption. The displacement of a program in favor of another offering of a planned (sporting events, parades) or unplanned (news event) nature.

Prime time. Varies locally, but is usually the three-hour period in which the network controls programming. In most time zones it is the period of 7 to 10 P.M.

Print. A photographed shot or sequence of sufficient quality to be developed and viewed for use in a film.

Production company. Today, an independent business which produces films or videotapes by renting space from a major studio.

Production hierarchy. The pecking order in a production, from the top down: network representative or office, executive producer, producer, director, assistant director.

Production office. The front office suite which serves as a headquarters for a series.

Ratings. The "bible" of television popularity. The A.C. Nielsen Company (and others of less importance) measures audience receptivity to programs and commercials. This information is sold to networks and producers to be used as the basis for setting advertising charges and—ultimately—discontinuing programs.

Representative. An agent. One who is responsible for finding work for his employers, the "talent."

Rewriting. The process of reworking a script, a job which goes on up to the moment of recording. It is a far more active process in electronic television than in filmed television or features.

Scene. A succession of interrelated shots which create a complete dramatic unit. See also "sequence."

Season. Usually twenty-six weeks; may be slightly less if preemptions for holidays and sporting events are taken into account. This period is under a constant state of revision as producers press to shorten the number of segments necessary to meet their contracts with networks. (In the 1950s, a "season" was thirty-six weeks long.)

Segment. One production in a series; a show.

Sequence. A series of interrelated shots comprising a complete dramatic unit. Normally, the plotting and dialogue of a sequence surround one main piece of action.

Set-up. A single, fixed position for a camera. Moving this camera, and the actors, to another location is termed a "reset."

Share. The percentage of a television audience that any program attracts; used with ratings.

Shot. The building-block of a sequence. One continuous run of film or tape which comprises a single action.

Show. Synonym: segment, production.

Single-camera technique. The basic technique of filmed television. One camera films all of the shots (i.e., masters and close-ups). Later, the films are edited together.

Special. An almost defunct expression referring to a single-presentation event, as distinct from a "series."

Standards and practices. Rules enforced by the network production office, whose job it is to make certain that specified actions and references are not used in scripts. For example, NBC-TV will not allow a crime to be shown in such a way that one could replicate the actions—at least, that is their expressed intent.

Studio. Any filmmaking firm, e.g., Universal Studios, the Burbank Studios, Warner Brothers Studios.

Sweetening. Adding laughter to a sound track. Usually done to cover edits or add "vitality" to a slow-moving moment in a script. A post-production process.

Talent. A synonym for actors.

TAT or Tandem Productions. Norman Lear and Bud Yorkin's production company.

Television movie. A long-form, single-presentation program; ordinarily, not made as a potential series.

Theatrical film. See "feature."

Treatment. A short version of a script, written descriptively rather than with dialogue.

Two-shot. A show containing two characters or subjects.

Type. As in "type-casting"; a stereotype. Actors often specialize in performing a limited range of characterizations, and are thus "type-cast."

Index